Joshua Parker, Ralph J. Poole (Eds.)

Austria and America: 20th-Century Cross-Cultural Encounters

American Studies in Austria

edited by

Astrid M. Fellner
(Saarland University)
Klaus Rieser
(University of Graz)
Hanna Wallinger
(University of Salzburg)

Volume 15

LIT

Austria and America:
20th-Century Cross-Cultural Encounters

edited by

Joshua Parker and Ralph J. Poole

LIT

Cover Image: Hugh M. Parker

Printed with the support of:

Stadt Salzburg
Universität Salzburg
STIFTUNGS- UND FÖRDERUNGSGESELLSCHAFT
DER PARIS-LODRON-UNIVERSITÄT SALZBURG

Bibliographic information published by the Deutsche Nationalbibliothek
The Deutsche Nationalbibliothek lists this publication in the Deutsche Nationalbibliografie; detailed bibliographic data are available on the Internet at http://dnb.d-nb.de.

ISBN 978-3-643-90812-4

A catalogue record for this book is available from the British Library

Klosbachstr. 107
CH-8032 Zürich
Tel. +41 (0) 44-251 75 05
E-Mail: zuerich@lit-verlag.ch   http://www.lit-verlag.ch
Distribution:
In the UK: Global Book Marketing, e-mail: mo@centralbooks.com
In North America: International Specialized Book Services, e-mail: orders@isbs.com
In Germany: LIT Verlag Fresnostr. 2, D-48159 Münster
Tel. +49 (0) 2 51-620 32 22, Fax +49 (0) 2 51-922 60 99, e-mail: vertrieb@lit-verlag.de
In Austria: Medienlogistik Pichler-ÖBZ, e-mail: mlo@medien-logistik.at
e-books are available at www.litwebshop.de

CONTENTS

INTRODUCTION

JOSHUA PARKER

If "austrianness," wrote Claudio Magris, "is the art of the fugue, of wandering, the love of pausing to wait for an ever-sought homeland which, as Schubert's vagabond says, may be approached, but never found" (282), American narrative identity, suggests Carra Glatt, involves "the essential loneliness of the American wanderer, who must pay so heavy a price for his forbidden seas and barbarous coasts" (43). The two met over several days in 2014 and 2015, as some thirty scholars, wandering near or far from home, joined for conferences on Austrian-American cultural relations from 1933 to the present in Salzburg's Stefan Zweig Centre. We wish to thank Klemens Renoldner and the Stefan Zweig Centre for hosting them. We wish to thank the City of Salzburg, the Stiftung Salzburg and the Stiftungs- und Förderungsgesellschaft der Paris-Lodron-Universität Salzburg for their interest in seeing this work in print, Karin Wohlgemuth for her help in securing funding, Judith Hartl for her help in typesetting, our Vice Rector of International Relations Sylvia Hahn, and all our colleagues in the University of Salzburg's history department whose work and presentations enriched our meetings in 2014 and 2015. "'Here it is!'" cried one of Lore Segal's Austrian-American returnees to Vienna, much like Walter Abish or Carl Djerassi themselves in the city of their childhood. To find one's memories physically embodied, Segal suggested, has "that odd little importance one feels in presenting certificationdriver's license, a library card" (*Her First American* 265).

"Austrian civilization," Magris wrote, after pondering history, place, international relations and central Europe, "claims itself either as a baroque totality transcending History, or as a post-historic crumbling or dispersion in the wake of modern history's rising tide." In either case, "it refuses purely historical criteria of evaluation, the measures of reference from which we normally attribute more or less priority to phenomenon, and class them by order of importance" (111). The same might be said of American civilization, as a lens from which to view all sorts of phenomenon–geographical, cultural, historical, artistic, literary, political. Austria and America perhaps both suffer from what Nick Danforth has recently called "imperial nostalgia," as America attempts to situate itself in a world that continues to spin after the "end of history" (Fukuyama).

"This is hardly a complicated story," Hermann Broch, a Viennese author exiled to the United States in 1938, opened one of his tales. "We'll dissolve its ingredients later, perhaps to be surprised at its simplicity. Or even more unsurprised, as we already know literature lives through just a very few, simple problems" (24). The protagonist of Peter Handke's *Short Letter, Long Farewell* (1972), while traveling across America, is reading *The Great Gatsby*. Handke dedicated his *Nachmittag eines Schriftstellers* (1987) to Fitzgerald in memory of Fitzgerald's "Afternoon of an Author" (1936), but Handke offers a cleverly succinct synopsis of the better-known American classic: "It is a love story about a man who buys a house on a bay for the sole purpose of seeing the lights go on every evening in a house on the other side of the bay" (9). These chapters likewise illuminate points on two sides of a physical and cultural distance, a space serving as both a barrier and a means of communication.

Jonathan W. Singerton begins with a reflection on the U.S. Embassy in Vienna's recent celebration of 175 years of official U.S.-Austrian diplomatic relations. His chapter suggests such diplomatic relations, well-deserving of commemoration, also deserve to have their timeline's curtain pulled back half a century in history for a look at William Lee's assignment as a hopeful diplomat to the Habsburg Court in Vienna in 1778. Jeanne Holland's "The Irony of Freud and the Americans: What Lies beneath the Surface" unpacks just why descendants of New England Puritans were so taken with Freudian theory at the turn of the century. Freud had a warm academic welcome to America, eventually helping draw new followers in the United States to his work and making it accessible to twentieth-century Americans for decades to come. Dean J. Kotlowski describes American reactions to the Third Reich's annexation of Austria in 1938, showing how the *Anschluss* played out in a Pacific region distant from both America and Austria, but in which each had a physical stake. The Philippines, where a large group of Austrian refugees had relocated, became a proxy battleground between the U.S. high commissioner there and German officials in the years before the United States officially entered the Second World War, and was a proxy battleground for Roosevelt's maneuvers against National Socialism's antisemitism.

Bernhard Wenzl takes up John Dos Passos's 1945 travel writing from the heart of central Europe in the months immediately after the War. The ruins he described would linger in the American imagination of postwar Austria–and indeed still do, as Anne-Marie Scholz describes in her discussion of Carol Reed's 1950 film, *The Third Man*. The film is as much ruin porn in visual images as Dos Passos's *Tour of Duty* (1946) is in verbal imagery. Yuval Lubin contrasts literature and film with a study of Stefan Zweig's novella *Letter from an Unknown Woman* (1922). Zweig's narrative was translated into film for American audiences a quarter of a century after its original publication. Its transformation, Lubin shows, reflects shifts from Austrian modernist sentiment to more romantic popular American culture. F.O. Matthiessen was one of the era's most thoughtful reflectors on postwar Europe and its hopes for a brighter future, and his story, as he returned home to a 1950s America of rising McCarthyism, would have been familiar to filmmaker Abraham Lincoln Polonsky, another American citizen hounded by the federal government, in part, ironically, for having been a strong opponent of European fascism. My chapter examines Polonsky's faith in both Marxian and Freudian theory, how Hollywood blacklisting led him to novel-writing in order to keep his audience, and his representations of Vienna and New York. Dante Mazzari reviews just how official U.S. policy toward Austria developed in the 1940s and 1950s, from Washington's perspective on shifting events and situations along the Iron Curtain's frontier, or indeed between its pleats.

The United States set up its State Department's Division of Cultural Affairs in 1938 in order to coordinate activities involving international cultural contacts, in part to compete with the Axis powers' propaganda (Wagnleitner 50). After the war, Austria may not have been denazified, but its theater, music and film industries were, beginning in 1947. The U.S. State Department showed itself eager to set up contacts between Austrian and American publishing houses (Wagnleitner 70). American press agencies were active in the creation of the Austrian Press Association in 1946, which made AP and Reuters central sources of foreign news in Austria. Domestic reporting, in term of style, if not content, was in turn influenced by the fact that hundreds of Austrian journalists had been trained in American-style journalism before the U.S. armed forces left the country in 1955 (Wagnleitner 100). Important as diplomatic, filmic, literary and scientific intersections between Austria and the United States were in the first half of the twentieth century, academic exchanges became essential to many encounters in the century's second half. Marty Gecek relates the history of American studies' originating base in postwar Europe. From Salzburg in

1947, her chapter turns to more cultural and academic, but no less diplomatic, exchanges, tracing the story of the Salzburg Seminar in American Studies, an institution that inspired and helped to form several generations of European Americanists, and whose outgrowing organizations continue to do so, now seventy years later.

One of an estimated 300,000 Austrian-born U.S. citizens (Spaulding 308), Carl Djerassi had an enormous influence on the lives of Americans, and indeed on American civilization. Walter Grünzweig's chapter shows Djerassi not only as a *Grenzgänger* between science and literature, but between nations, working in the American West before returning late in life to his native land to indulge, as he himself humorously noted, in the cuisine of his childhood with something like Proustian nostalgia, the "weight-conscious lipophobic Californian" in him drawing back in horror even as "the Viennese" in him salivates. The Californian and the Viennese in Djerassi are never quite reconciled, leaving him with something like the "double vision" of Austrian-American author Walter Abish, which Marta Koval's chapter discusses. Austrians in America, like the protagonists of William Gass's *Middle C* (2013), which Koval's chapter also treats, often find themselves floating between two distinct visions of their environment, or even of themselves. Returning to Austria as adults, they often experience equally disorienting sensations of uncanny recognition. As Djerassi suggested, childhood memories can sometimes only be seen through a dusty lens, the picture patchy. Remembering, Lore Segal wrote, as Freud's, Zweig's, Reed's, Abish's, Gass's and Djerassi's work all shows, "is a complicated act." There is "that coincidence of the ghostly, transparent, unstable stuff memory is made of, with the hard-edged material object, which, as often as not, is, in fact, altered." And there is "the degree of history the viewer shares with the view" (*Her First American* 265). A tissue of memories associated with new places is, she imagined, "the way our histories become charged thus upon the air, the streets, the very houses" (*Other People's Houses* 311-12), whether of New York or Vienna.

WORKS CITED

175 Years of U.S.-Austrian Diplomatic Relations: 1838-2013. Vienna: U.S. Embassy Vienna, 2013.

Broch, Herman. "Ophelia." *Novellen*. Frankfurt am Main: Suhrkamp, 1980. 24-36.

Danforth, Nick. "Imperial Nostalgia: Who Did It Better—And Why It Matters." *Foreign Affairs*. 19 Aug. 2015. Web.

Fukuyama, Francis. "The End of History?" *The National Interest*, Summer 1989: 3-18.

Glatt, Carra. "Proxy Narrative in *The Ambassadors*: Reconfiguring James's Ending." *Narrative* 24.1 (2016): 28-49.

Handke, Peter. *Short Letter, Long Farewell*. 1972. Trans. Ralph Manheim. New York: Farrar, Straus and Giroux, 1974.

—. *Nachmittag eines Schriftstellers*. Salzburg and Vienna: Residenz Verlag, 1987.

Magris, Claudio. *Danube*. Trans. Jean and Marie Noëlle Pastureau. Paris: Gallimard, 1988.

Segal, Lore. *Other People's Houses*. 1964. New York and London: The New P, 1990.

—. *Her First American*. 1985. New York and London: The New P, 2004.

Spaulding, E. Wilder. *The Quiet Invaders: The Story of the Austrian Impact Upon America*. Vienna: Österreichischer Bundesverlag für Unterricht, Wissenschaft und Kunst, 1968.

Wagnleitner, Reinhold. *Coca-Colonization and the Cold War: The Cultural Mission of the United States in Austria after the Second World War*. Chapel Hill: U of North Carolina P, 1994.

175 OR 235 YEARS OF AUSTRIAN-AMERICAN RELATIONS? REFLECTIONS AND REPERCUSSIONS FOR THE MODERN DAY[1]

JONATHAN W. SINGERTON

A feature common to both Austrians and Americans is the love of celebrating the past. The year 2015, for example, witnessed the 150th anniversary of the opening of the famous Ringstrasse in Vienna and at the same time marked the sesquicentennial of the American Civil War. 2017 will witness the 300th anniversary of Maria Theresa and the 100th anniversary of John F. Kennedy. It is no surprise then, that during 2013 the governments of the Republic of Austria and the United States of America seized the opportunity to celebrate the 175th anniversary of diplomatic relations between the two nations.

This celebration reflected the beginning of the Austrian-American relationship with the exchange of representatives in 1838. For the occasion the U.S. Embassy in Vienna developed a multimedia exhibition to demonstrate the tenacity of the relationship. It was comprised of a series of panels filled with historical memorabilia, a printed booklet, an accompanying video (with the coincidental timing of 17.5 minutes), and even commemorative mugs filled with Tootsie Rolls—the invention, we were reminded, of an Austrian-American.

Events were held throughout Austria, from Innsbruck in the West to Klagenfurt in the South. The most extravagant was held at the Diplomatic Academy in Vienna with then U.S. Ambassador William C. Eacho and Federal President of Austria Heinz Fischer in attendance. Both sides recounted how their lives have been shaped by the strong interrelation of Austria and the United States in the twentieth century, but in his remarks Ambassador Eacho noted how "From the outset, we knew it would be impossible to compile a full historical documentation of the relationship."

---

[1] The author wishes to thank his supervisors, Professor Francis D. Cogliano, Dr. David Silkenat, and Dr. David Kaufman at the University of Edinburgh for their support and gratefully acknowledges the generosity of the Dietrich W. Botstiber Foundation and the Institute of Austrian-American Studies which made the archival research for this chapter and the wider doctoral project possible.

"Our intention," he continued, "is to focus on the building, and at times, rebuilding of this relationship which has brought us to the continued cooperation and recognition of shared values on which our two countries thrive today."

Perhaps these comments help to explain the most glaring omission in the celebration of Austrian-American relations: the founding period itself. Whilst the 2013 anniversary commemorated 1838, this is only the official date that relations began. The real story of Austrian-American, or rather U.S.-Habsburg, relations extends some sixty years earlier. This period witnessed with the first diplomatic attempts between the Habsburg Monarchy and the new American republic starting with the mission of William Lee to Vienna in 1778 and ending with the five-year mission of Baron Frederick Eugene de Beelen-Bertholf from 1784-1789. These missions and this period are the focus of this chapter but are sadly something that has, until now, received relatively little historical and popular attention. The lack of inclusion of this earlier interaction into the official commemoration has compounded this state of scholarly and popular amnesia. As a consequence our historical understanding of the founding of the United States in Europe is still incomplete, our vision of the Habsburg Monarchy is limited, and naturally how we view Austrian-American relations today is overtly narrowed by this omission. It is for these reasons that we should ask ourselves: should we be celebrating 175 years or 235 years of Austrian-American relations?

"A STORY OF BENIGN NEGLECT"

This chapter aims to bring to light the relevance and richness of eighteenth-century U.S.-Habsburg relations despite their marginalisation both in popular and scholarly circles. In addition, it considers how reinstating this historical narrative alters our understanding of the present-day Austrian-American relationship. This should not only provide us with a greater insight into the history of Austrian-American relations but at the same time reveal something about the current relationship which, to borrow the phrase of Günter Bischoff, typically consists of "the American giant and the Austrian dwarf" (Bischoff 167).

When we turn to the eighteenth century, however, we find this situation reversed. It was Austria, as a component of the vast Habsburg Monarchy, that was the giant; and in 1776, the dwarf was the newly declared—but far from independent—United States of America. It was under these circumstances that the original effort to establish a diplomatic dialogue between the two states was first attempted. From the American perspective, the resolution to create a 'separate and equal station' for the thirteen colonies required the acknowledgement of other states in order to gain political legitimacy and international validity. The exigencies of the war with Great Britain also necessitated trade with foreign powers for war supplies not readily available on the American continent such as gunpowder and military uniforms. The Habsburg Monarchy had the potential to serve all these needs of the American confederacy and more. Joseph II's dual role as Holy Roman Emperor would also benefit the Americans, who sorely needed to supress the British procurement of German mercenaries. Thus the appointment of William Lee as envoy to the Courts of Vienna and Berlin on 1 July, 1777 was made with these aims in mind: to propose a treaty of friendship, establish necessary commerce and to utilise the Habsburg position to quell the flow of Hessian troops into British ranks. It is important to remember then that it was the American dwarf which first reached out towards the Habsburg giant.

The challenge presented to the American 'militia diplomats' was staggering, especially as they were breaking the traditional conventions of European diplomacy by soliciting at courts uninvited. As an unrecognised state in the throes of revolutionary turmoil and amid a war against one of the greatest sovereign powers in Europe, the American diplomats could not have been on a less equal footing with those in the European circles, most of all at the highly dynastic Habsburg court in Vienna. The choice of William Lee as envoy did not help matters. Though no stranger to pageantry from his time as Sheriff and later Alderman of the City of London, Lee was neither a nobleman nor a diplomat and was completely unfamiliar with the conduct of Viennese society. To make matters worse, he spoke little French and no German whatsoever. So how did revolutionaries think the 'American dwarf' could win over the 'Habsburg giant' onto their side?

These circumstances should excite us as scholars, as historians, but most of all as Austro-Americanists. After all, they echo the words of Lonnie Johnson, the current director of the Austrian-American Fulbright programme, who said during the 2013 anniversary: "The [most] interesting thing about Austrian-American relations is of course the asymmetries which exist between a very very large superpower and a small state." The same is true for the eighteenth century as today. Yet this feature has failed to capture the fascination of numerous historians, especially those of the American Revolution. One academic, for example, recently summarised the situation: "If you teach a survey course on the history of American foreign relations, chances are that you don't spend very much time on the Habsburg Empire. As Rodney Dangerfield may have put it, the Habsburgs get no respect" (Schwartz 6).

This lack of 'respect' for the Habsburg element in early American diplomacy has been particularly acute in American scholarship, where the most comprehensive work in English appeared in 1978, two hundred years after Lee's mission, by Karl Roider in the *Virginia Magazine of History and Biography*. Roider's assessment, however, failed to appreciate the numerous perspectives through which we can view Lee's mission and the different ways to measure its success. Instead the focus on wider geopolitical events in Europe and the personal deficiencies of William Lee as a diplomat skew the conclusion towards one centred on a failure of the mission. This obscures the fact that there was substantial interest for the American Revolution and its agent in Vienna and without being able to discern such interest, we are left with a false impression of outright rejection of both William Lee and American revolutionary ideals by the Habsburgs in 1778. The real story, in essence, was not as straightforward as we may think. This more complicated—and ultimately more intriguing—Habsburg reaction has not only been downplayed but has also come to dominate American interpretations of this early relationship. Historians such as Samuel Flagg Bemis, Jonathan R. Dull and Richard Morris have all emphasised an icy diplomatic climate that Lee unsuccessfully confronted in Vienna.

A similar supposition can be found amongst the conclusions of German-speaking academics such as, for example, Anna H. Benna and Paula S. Fichtner. The preliminary research completed by Hans Schlitter as head of the *Haus-Hof-und-Staatsarchiv* in Vienna towards the end of the nineteenth-century points to a rich body of evidence but fails to situate an analysis in a balanced and unbiased way.[2] Horst Dippel in his groundbreaking work *Germany and the American Revolution, 1770-1800* (1977) contributes to this sense of malaise by stating: "The sporadic appearance of American negotiators in Vienna and Berlin does not seem to have had any noteworthy influence" (39). Perhaps the most damning overall verdict is given by Rudolf Agstner in one of the few monographs to deal solely with the diplomatic

[2] Likewise Rudolf Friebel's doctoral dissertation completed at the University of Innsbruck in 1955 largely follows the research and conclusions of Schlitter.

development between Austria and America, where the entire 1778-1838 period is summarised in two pages under the description 'a story of benign neglect' (36)—a title which perhaps reflects rather more the scholarly apathy than the contemporary events themselves.

How historians have viewed the past shapes the public recollections around this period, and it is evident to see this sense of neglect transpire from academic circles. The booklet compiled by the Public Affairs Department of the U.S. Embassy and issued during the 2013 celebration, for example, gave an overview of this period in just two paragraphs. In November 2013 an article appeared in the *Vienna Review* with the title "New World Rebels at the Imperial Court," which noted how William Lee and his colleagues were not referred to as 'Americans' but rather 'rebels' and 'insurgents' by the Habsburg court, further perpetuating the myth of Viennese hostility towards the American cause (Ballman). Altogether this is indicative of how academic and public impressions of this period have focused on a foregone conclusion: Austrian-American relations in 1778 amount to nothing surprising since the Habsburg court proved to be adverse and unwilling to accept an illegitimate diplomat who could not carry out his duties effectively.

AN AMERICAN IN VIENNA

Contrary to these current historical beliefs, William Lee, whilst in Vienna, excitedly penned to his younger brother Arthur on 10 June 1778, "Some of distinction, however, are warm for the part of America" (Ford 444). Lee's remark is insightful as it points us towards a truer sense of the Habsburg reaction to and reception of the American Revolution. In fact, the research presented here reveals how there were indeed numerous American sympathisers spread amongst the Habsburg echelons of power and across the dominions of the Empire.

The greatest proponent of American events in Vienna was arguably Dr. Jan Ingenhousz, who served as the court physician and a personal confidant to Maria Theresa. Since 1764 Ingenhousz had become friends with the most famous American in Europe, Benjamin Franklin, and the pair maintained a frequent correspondence that spanned fifteen years between 1773-1788 (Brewer-Anderson and Conley 276-96). This friendship gave Ingenhousz unrivalled knowledge on American events, and as court interest intensified during the revolution period, he continually asked Franklin for news of the latest developments which he then "handed on in reports to Maria Theresa and other government officials" (Dippel 62).[3] In 1777 he articulated his sympathies for the American cause and defended Franklin during his humiliating treatment in the Cockpit by Tory ministers in a work entitled *Remarques sur les affaires presente de l'Amérique*. In this treatise Ingenhousz dispelled the spurious notions of Franklin-devised colonial conspiracy and argued that the defence of American rights were a matter for all of Europe to be concerned with, especially the Habsburgs (HHStA, W443).

As a result, Ingenhousz quickly became an authority on America amongst Habsburg courtiers. An entry in the diary of Count Karl von Zinzendorf attests to Ingenhousz's significant notoriety, as he noted as early as 3 October 1775 that "I talked with Ingenhousz about the colonies, [and] he explained the origins of the conflict to me." Indeed Zinzendorf's highly detailed and lifelong diary provides an insight into the interests and sympathies of the numerous Habsburg courtiers, who absorbed American texts despite censorship. In the very week that William Lee arrived in Vienna, for example, Zinzendorf started reading John Dickinson's *Letters of a Farmer,* which was after he had devoured "that American pamphlet Common Sense which was written to draw fire against the King of England" (HHStA, Zinzendorf Tagebücher, 16 and 30 May 1778). The cause of bloodshed at the Battle of Lexington and Concord, Zinzendorf concluded, was due to the unjust "attempts of the British government to tax the colonists at will" (Zinzendorf, 3 October 1775).

Many of these sympathisers become visible to us precisely because of William Lee's visit to Vienna in May-July 1778. Despite his linguistic deficiencies, Lee became the star attraction at several dinner parties held by Austrian officials and his host Louis Auguste le Tonnelier, the Baron de Breteuil who as the French ambassador was able to entertain in a certain style of magnificence. From these dinners, Lee became well acquainted with Viennese aristocracy, whose first impressions fixated on how "rich, thoroughly ugly, [and] marked by the smallpox" the Virginian was (Schlitter 7).[4]

---

[3] Among these items we find Ingenhousz's French translation of Franklin's *Comparison of Great Britain and the United States in Regard to the Basis of Credit in the Countries* dated from 1777 and several letters translated into French for the perusal of Maria Theresa, today housed at the Österreichische National Bibliothek in Vienna.

[4] See the letters exchanged between Count Franz-Xaver Koller and Princess Anna Khevenhüller-Metsch, especially 28 May 1778.

Court letters gossiping about these dinner parties reveal how numerous sympathisers "continuously questioned the said American about hundreds of things of his country" and conversations centred on whether "there were a lot of deer [or wild boar] in America" (Koller to Khevenhüller-Metsch, 1 June 1778).

This surprising success riled the British ambassador in Vienna, Sir Robert Murray Keith, who informed his superiors and King George that "It has been a matter of great uneasiness to me, to remark within these few Days, that the Treatment of Mr Lee is very much changed in his Favour, and that he has not only been well received in several Visits to Count Colloredo, but that he has dined with very large Companies" (Keith to Earl Suffolk, 13 June 1778). Lee's mission became a severe antagonism to Keith, whose aim it was to bring the Habsburgs into the British fold and so Keith bolstered the Habsburg resolve of neutrality. As Lee made successive inroads with the help of Breteuil into the Habsburg political scene, Keith became ever more worrisome and begged his superiors in London for more adequate instructions in how to deal with the formidable American envoy. Though Maria Theresa eventually denied Lee an audience, Lee's visits to the court at Schönbrunn and his friendship the palace's chamberlain, Count Hatzfeld, unnerved Keith greatly. Even though the State Chancellor Prince Wenzel Anton von Kaunitz reportedly never spoke a word, the actual meeting between Kaunitz and Lee–arranged through Breteuil's pretence of presenting a foreign traveller–sent Keith into a flurry of panic as he sought assurances from the State Chancellor that Lee would be completely isolated.

News of Lee's visit had even impacted further afield in the Habsburg Empire. The Bohemian-born Professor at the Imperial Academy in Buda, Hungary, Johann (also János) Zinner came to Vienna around September 1778 purposefully to meet with William Lee. Disappointed to learn that Lee had in fact left for Berlin in July, Zinner wrote to Benjamin Franklin in Paris instead. In his letter dating from October 1778, he asked for information on America for two of his forthcoming books: both to be written in Latin and entitled *Historical Notes on the United Colonies in America* and *About Some Illustrious Americans*.[5] Despite the fact that Franklin complied with Zinner's request, these books have never been found. Fortunately, in 1782 Zinner published a work in German entitled *Merkwürdige Briefe und Schriften der berühmtesten Generäle in America*, which drew from the same material and

[5] In Latin: *Notitia Historica de Coloniss Foederatis in Americae* and *De Viris Illustribus Americae.*

gave an accompanying biography to each major American figure of the Revolution across some three hundred pages. Before the American Revolution war was over, Zinner had created one of its most detailed and earliest accounts.

Although Zinner explained his work was not a political manifesto—likely from fear of censorship—it helped to galvanise respect and interest for the American cause across the Habsburg lands (Halácsy 12-13). In his letter to Franklin, Zinner expressed his sincerest sentiments of support for the American cause. "I was born the subject of a great monarchy," he wrote, "and under a government whose rule is mild [...] but I cannot tell you what joy I feel, when I hear or read of your progress in America. To speak the truth, I look upon you and all the chiefs of your new republic, as angels, sent by heaven to guide and comfort the human race... [and] to give a public manifestation of this sentiment, I am composing these works" (Jean-Claude de Zinner to Benjamin Franklin, 18 October 1778).

Viennese newspapers acted as the largest conduit of information. No paper had direct correspondence with America, so news was adapted from other German papers, which in turn were informed by publications in London or Paris, meaning that "even under the most favourable conditions an American event could be known about in about six weeks after its occurrence" (Zaker 31-32). Yet the most prolific newspaper on American events was the *Wienerisches Diarium*. The twice-weekly publication was the most circulated in Habsburg lands and held the privilege of being the official state newspaper. The *Diarium* reported on three disturbances between Britain and her colonies, though always superficially and without comment; partly from censorship but also due to the scarcity of reliable sources (*Wienerisches Diarium*, 7 April, 7 July, and 26 September 1770). American events, however, consistently featured in the output of the newspaper. Strikingly, none of these publications contained any mention of Lee's mission, perhaps at the insistence of the Habsburg censors or authorities.

Viennese readers, however, became familiar with leading figures like Benjamin Franklin, John Adams and John Hancock but precision naturally suffered from sources that were "inaccurate, incomplete, or simply propaganda" (Dippel 17). The most notable errors concerned George Washington—the supposed "Dictator of the American Estates"—who received several premature obituaries throughout his lifetime (*WD*, 26 August 1775). Despite misinformation, the Viennese papers proved unusually perceptive at times. Early on the conclusion was drawn that "the rigid attitudes of both sides [means] war can hardly be avoided" (*WD*, 11 Feb. 1775). Vienna therefore was far more receptive to the Americans than we might expect. Even when the two nations existed under diametrically opposed political systems—one monarchical, the other republican—there existed a considerable fascination within the Habsburg realms that intensified during and after the War of American Independence.

This fascination was partly fanned by the political aspects of the American Revolution but was in larger part stoked by the American celebrity Benjamin Franklin. News of Franklin's return to Europe in December 1776 reached Vienna shortly afterwards.[6] His notoriety as an inventor and scientist far outstripped his commissioner colleagues and earned him the respect of the Habsburg monarch Joseph II who had previously read an Italian translation of Franklin's work (Pace 26).[7] So taken in by the New World savant was the Emperor Joseph II that he attempted to meet with Franklin personally during his tour through France and visit to his sister Queen Marie Antoinette in Paris in 1777. Franklin received his invitation to drink hot chocolate with Count Falkenstein—the Emperor's alias—on Wednesday 28 May through the secretary of the Tuscan delegation, Abbé Raimondo Niccoli. However, both Franklin and the Emperor were to be disappointed, as Franklin's recollection informs us that "The Emperor did not appear, and the Abbé since tells me that the number of other persons who occasionally visited him that morning [...] prevented his coming... [however] at twelve [...] he came but I was gone" (Victory 26). It is unknown why Joseph did not arrange further attempts to meet with Franklin.

If Joseph had met with Franklin that day, it might have wrecked the coherency of Chancellor Kaunitz's policy of neutrality. As with William Lee in Vienna, the acceptance of an American agent's presence before the Habsburg monarch would confer a level of legitimacy on the agents still officially referred to as 'rebels' by the court. From 1776-1779 the Habsburgs constructed an initial neutrality aimed at avoiding any actions that might disturb the delicate politics of Europe. After all, a fragile truce with Prussia had only just been secured following the War of Bavarian Succession, which diplomatically could have become caught up with the colonial dispute and resulted in a wider conflagration similar to the previous outbreak of the

[6] Although with some inaccuracies: "*Dr Franklin ist ein Greis von 84 Jahren, aber von solcher Munterkeit, dass man ihn kaum für einen 60-jährigen Mann ansieht*" (*WD* 1 Jan. 1777). Franklin's actual age at this point was 71.

[7] The pamphlet was written by Giambatista Toderini, and entitled *Filosofia Frankliniana.*

Seven Years' War. Kaunitz and the monarchs felt this possibility, especially as they became increasingly alarmed by their French ally's meddling with the American situation. Diplomatic neutrality and non-recognition of the Americans became the only viable way to avoid a wider conflict in Europe. Thus the Habsburgs solidified their position behind an ideological imperative that other monarchs could not violate the domestic sovereignty of others. "The cause in which England is engaged," Emperor Joseph reportedly feigned, "is the cause of all sovereigns, who have a joint interest in the maintenance of due subordination and obedience to law in all the surrounding monarchies. I observe with pleasure the vigorous exertions of the national strength, which the King [of England] is employing to bring his rebellious subjects to submission, and I sincerely wish success to the measures" (Roider 126). Joseph's rebuke was as much a scathing criticism of French policy as it was reassurance to the British.

A HABSBURG IN PHILADELPHIA

No existing work fully encapsulates the Habsburg position following this point in 1779. Yet in some sense this is when U.S.-Habsburg relations become more dynamic, and so a much richer picture develops if we go beyond this point. Despite the construction of a policy of neutrality supported by the Habsburg entrance into the Russian plan of Armed Neutrality in the War of American Independence, this Habsburg neutrality was slowly eroded by the close of the war with the Treaty of Paris in 1783. Following the entry of Spain and the Dutch Republic into the war against Britain, the Habsburgs feared the consequences that a dismembered British Empire and fully realised Bourbon victory could have for the balance of power in Europe. Mindful of these concerns and seeking to avenge the humiliation suffered from French arbitration in the Treaty of Teschen in 1779, the Habsburgs were compelled to act. Thus Austria twice offered mediation in the negotiation of peace in the War of American Independence.

Commercial interests intensified with the prospect of peace and a previously exclusive British market in the Americas becoming open to European traders. As early as 7 August 1776, Captain Christoph Heller informed the Court Commerce Chamber in Vienna that "the current situation of the English colonies in America seems to me to merit considerable attention, namely to earn more than ever before… and to have commerce, which has especially made the Dutch and English so rich and respectable" (FHKA, NHK, Kommerz Abt., Noten, K. 616). Lobbyists continued to emerge through the War of American Independence such as the Swiss-born merchant Zollikofer von Sonnenberg who proposed establishing a trade route from the Habsburg possessions on the Adriatic coast in the Mediterranean to the North American ports, though Kaunitz—still uncertain of the fate of the new American states—resolved that "Since the trade with North America of the hereditary lands presents no such significant advantage [...] this application should be dismissed" (Kaunitz to Joseph II, 30 June 1782).

The Habsburg desire to remain neutral until the conclusion of peace had already been tested earlier in 1782 following the rise in the amount of smuggling and use of the neutral Habsburg naval flag. Though one among many such cases, the incarceration of the ship *Den Eersten* belonging to an Ostend company trading out of the Austrian Netherlands by an American ship, the *Hope*, caused serious concern. The impounded cargo was taken to Boston and the crew were tried for smuggling contraband under false pretences. As the case reached the New England admiralty courts, the distressed merchant owners of the ship back in the Austrian Netherlands sought aid through the most renowned American advocate in Europe, Benjamin Franklin, who was now negotiating peace in Paris. Franklin discussed the matter with the Austrian ambassador Count Mercy-D'Argenteau, suggesting "If his Imperial Majesty should think fit to appoint a Consul General to reside in those States, such an officer might at all times assist his Compatriots with his Consels and Protection in any Affairs they might have in that Country [the United States]." Franklin urged this prospect further by insinuating that "I apprehend these Cases may hereafter be frequent; and if the Complaints are to be addressed to you & to me, we are likely to have a great deal of trouble" (Franklin to Mercy-D'Argenteau, 31 March 1782).

Franklin in essence was washing his hands of the case but his suggestion to the Habsburgs had a greater resonance and ministers in Vienna and Brussels considered how to keep their valuable trade links with the emerging United States open after the expected peace treaties had been signed. Mercy-D'Argenteau relayed Franklin's suggestion to his superiors. The Habsburg Governor of the Austrian Netherlands, Prince Georg Adam von Starhemberg, noted how this action and the case itself would trap the Habsburgs into recognising American sovereignty and legal legitimacy before the settlement of the peace process. "There can be no discussion," he concluded, "so long as the fate of the colonies remains undecided" (Starhemberg to Mercy-

D'Argenteau, 31 May 1782). The Habsburgs were unwilling to recognise the American states in their own independent rights until they had been sanctioned by international agreement.

However, the idea of Habsburg representation and the possibility of acquiring American trade took root and precipitated a rapid U-turn in Habsburg policy towards America between 1782 and 1783. The former Habsburg ambassador in London and future successor to Prince Starhemberg in the Austrian Netherlands, Graf Ludwig von Barbiano-Belgiojoso, saw potential in the American markets for the Austrian holdings in the Netherlands, especially as the Dutch had held an advantage through entering the American war earlier and having long closed the River Scheldt to Austrian shipping. American trade would not only be a lucrative venture for the Monarchy but they would risk falling behind if they did not partake in the commercial action. With the Peace of Paris being finalised, the Habsburgs acted. Belgiojoso reported to Kaunitz that Mercy-D'Argenteau urged, "Through decorous insinuations to the American Ministers in Paris, to send immediately empowered representatives to Vienna. Therewith all possible and preparatory introductions and measures for a trade-nexus between the Hereditary Lands and the American States can be made with little time lost as possible" (Belgiojoso to Kaunitz, 19 March 1783).

Meanwhile, Kaunitz entertained a rather unusual guest in Vienna, a 'creole' by the name of du Roissy from St. Dominique who had made the journey to solicit the appointment of a trade delegate to the new independent American States (Benna 10; Joseph II to Kaunitz March 18th 1783). Now seeing the merit in establishing a Habsburg stake in the American markets, Kaunitz enlisted Jan Ingenhousz to write persistently to Franklin offering him an official visit to Vienna and making clear the Emperor's warm feelings towards the United States. At the same time, Count Mercy-D'Argenteau paid one of the American commissioners in Paris, John Adams, a visit. Enthused by the Habsburg ambassador's surprise visit, Adams wrote immediately to Congress relaying how they "ran over a variety of Subjects, particularly the Commerce which might take place, between the United States and Germany, by the way of Trieste & Fiume" (Adams to President of Congress, 3 July 1783). These measures were a brilliant coordination of a suddenly new Habsburg policy towards America.

Likewise, these Habsburg ports on the Adriatic felt the buzz for new American ventures and commercial opportunity. Throughout the eighteenth century many Habsburgs merchants had expanded their horizons towards the

Orient and the far reaches of the Mediterranean, now their appetites stretched across the Atlantic. One company in particular, Belletti and Zaccar, based in Trieste, sought to capitalise on American opportunities before the United States had even been officially recognised by the Peace of Paris. Aware of the delicate situation, the co-owner, Dominique-Francois Belletti, wrote several times in early 1783 to Benjamin Franklin, informing him that "our company intends an expedition of a ship under imperial colours to Philadelphia with products and manufactures of our state and of the Levant" (Belletti to Franklin, 11 April 1783). Belletti tasked Franklin with issuing letters of recommendations for the company's captain for his arrival in Philadelphia but, understandably preoccupied in Paris by the peace negotiations, Franklin failed to comply. Desperate, Belletti's additional requests also fell on Franklin's deaf ears even as Belletti included a signed letter of support from the then current Governor of Trieste, the American sympathiser Count Karl von Zinzendorf. Regardless of Franklin's silence, Belletti and Zaccar's ship arrived in Philadelphia by the end of 1783 and by Wednesday 10 December an advertisement appeared in the local Gazette for "Zant and Sicily Currants, Smyrna Raizins [and] Turkey Figs of excellent quality" sold on behalf of the company. The first post-war U.S.-Habsburg commercial exchange had occurred just over three months after the United States had full gained international legitimacy with the Treaty of Paris.

Franklin, however, did respond to his friend Jan Ingenhousz. Though he turned down the prospect of a mission to Vienna citing ill health, Franklin made another influential suggestion for the Habsburgs: "My best advice to your commercial People, is to send over a discreet, intelligent Person with instructions to travel thro' the [United States and] observe the Nature of the Commerce" (Franklin to Ingenhousz, 16 May 1783). The Habsburg court followed Franklin's "best advice" and settled on a middle-rank bureaucrat and noble from the Brabant Department in the Austrian Netherlands, Baron Frederick Eugene de Beelen-Berthoff. Though Kaunitz had reservations about whether Beelen's economic knowledge of the Habsburg hereditary lands was sufficient, it was said that Beelen had "enough spirit and talent to oversee the post of a hardworking councillor and advisor" (Schlitter 77). In 1783, Beelen set sail for the American capital of Philadelphia on the same ship that carried Professor Franz Joseph Märter, who led a botanic expedition to the southern United States, and both carried recommendations signed by Franklin.

Although he was not formally received, Baron de Beelen was sent as the first individual in the US-Habsburg relationship to carry out his representative mission successfully. His priority was to monitor the level of commercial activity in the new country for the next several years and to assess the suitability for further Habsburg trade. In addition, and following on from Franklin's other suggestion, Beelen was officially designated to deal with any maritime legal issues that Habsburg vessels might encounter, acting as a representative or official commercial advisor. Some fifty-five years before the exchange of U.S.-Habsburg representatives in 1838, Beelen in essence performed a role similar to that of a consul. Yet he also went far beyond this brief. His regular and voluminous reports contained a vast source of information about the state of the young nation which were not merely limited to Philadelphia's trade but included information about the commercial and political developments of many states from Massachusetts in the North to Georgia in the South.[8]

Beelen also seems to have successfully integrated himself into the American social fabric of the day, though further research is needed to clarify to what extent. He was, for example, made a member of the American Philosophical Society in 1785—the same year as Thomas Jefferson. Beelen's reports also detail his acquaintance with many prominent American leaders such as Richard Henry Lee, the original proponent of the Declaration of Independence, elder brother of William Lee, and then President of Congress from 1784 to 1785. Perhaps it is because of these connections that Beelen felt compelled or confident enough, upon the expiration of his duties and consequent recall, to disavow the Habsburg authorities as he refused to return to Europe citing his ill health. Beelen and his family eventually settled in rural Lancaster County, Pennsylvania. There, he helped to establish a church along the banks of the River Conewago, where today Beelen and his American familial descendants are still interred.

[8] Beelen's reports are today housed at the *Haus-Hof-und-Staatsarchiv* in Vienna under the 'Belgien Berichte' series, as they were originally transmitted first to Brussels before the court in Vienna.

Beelen's Grave Today at Cemetery of the Conewago Chapel, Adams County, Pennsylvania
(Taken by the author, 28 June 2015)

CONCLUDING THOUGHTS

What does this mean for the modern-day relationship? In 2013 former President Fischer remarked, "175 years of history is not a young friendship, it is a long historical relation." To extend this by a further sixty years only heightens our understanding by encompassing the entirety of the longer historical interactions and their legacies between Austria and America. The earlier U.S.-Habsburg period reinforces this to an even greater extent. It is no surprise then that the gift Ambassador Eacho presented to President Fischer at Diplomatic Academy celebrations was a copy of Benjamin Franklin's 1777 letter to Count Mercy-D'Argenteau, notifying the Habsburg court of the intention to send William Lee as envoy to Vienna. The first interactions, successful or not, still have resonance for us today and so the first attempt cannot be forgotten if a proper sense of the current relationship is to be made. President Fischer's response was to note how the "The United States stood at the cradle of the Austrian Republic twice." I would only add that we cannot forget that it was Austria which was also present at the birth of the United States, as well.

WORKS CITED

ONLINE SOURCES:

William C. Eacho, Ambassador's Speech at the 175 Years Gala on 13 February 2013. <http://austria.usembassy.gov/amb-speeches/175.html>

Heinz Fischer, Federal President of Austria Remarks given at the 175 Years Gala on 13 February 2013. <https://www.youtube.com/watch?v=i-tfsNWUEUg>

Lonnie Johnson, Director of the Austrian-American Fulbright Programme, 175 Year Celebration Videos, uploaded 20 Nov. 2013 <https://www.youtube.com/watch?v=tREFYm0BuxM>

Wienerisches Diarium <http://anno.onb.ac.at/cgi-content/anno?aid=wrz> [1.03.2012]

UNPUBLISHED ARCHIVAL SOURCES:

Haus-Hof-und-Staatsarchiv, Vienna—
Belgien Berichte, DDB Rot 182a-e.
Frankreich Berichte, K. 7, 150, 155-68, Varia.
Staatskanzlei, Vorträge K. 38, 125, 137, 158.
Weisungen 443.
Tagebuch Zinzendorf—Band XXI

Finanz und Hofkammerarchiv, Vienna—
Kommerz Abt., K. 616, fols. 365-67.

National Archives at Kew, London—
Letterbook of Sir Robert Murray Keith, SP80-220.

PRINTED PRIMARY SOURCES:

Ford, Worthington C. ed. *Letters of William Lee.* I-II (New York, 1891)

U.S. Public Affairs Office—U.S. Embassy Vienna."175 Years of Austrian-American Diplomatic Relations" (Vienna, 2013).

UNPUBLISHED DISSERTATIONS:

Friebel, Rudolf. *Österreich und die Vereinigten Staaten bis zum Gesandaustausch im Jahre 1838.* Diss: Innsbruck, 1955.

Victory, Beatrice M. *Benjamin Franklin and Germany.* Diss: University of Pennsylvania, 1926.

SECONDARY SOURCES:

Agstner, Rudolf. *Austria(-Hungary) and Its Consulates in the United States of America.* Vienna: Lit Verlag, 2012.

Ballman, Simon. "New World Rebels at the Imperial Court." *The Vienna Review* 22 Nov. 2013.

Bemis, Samuel F. *A Diplomatic History of the United States*. New York: Holt, 1936.

Benna, Anna H. *Contemporary Austrian Views of American Independence: A Documentary on the Occasion of the Bicentennial*. Trans. C. Bernard. Vienna: Böhlau Verlag, 1976.

Bischoff, Günter. "Of Dwarfs and Giants–From Cold War Mediator to Bad Boy of Europe: Austria and the U.S. in the Transatlantic Arena (1990-2013)." *Relationships-Beziehungsgeschichten–Austria and the United States in the Twentieth Century*. Innsbruck: Studien Verlag, 2014. 167-95.

Brewer-Anderson, Melissa and Conley, Timothy K. "Franklin and Ingenhousz: A Correspondence of Interests." *Proceedings of the American Philosophical Society* 141.3 (Sept. 1997): 276-96.

Dippel, Horst. *Germany and the American Revolution 1770-1800–A Sociohistorical Investigation of Late Eighteenth-century Political Thinking*. Trans. B. Uhlendorf. Williamsburg: Institute of Early American History and Culture, 1977

Dull, Jonathan R. *A Diplomatic History of the American Revolution*. New Haven: Yale UP, 1985.

Fichtner, Paula S. "Viennese Perspectives on the American War of Independence." Eds. Király, Béla K. and Barany, George. *East Central European Perceptions of Early America*. Dordrecht: The Peter de Ridder P, 1977: 19-32.

Halácsy, Katalin. "The Image of Benjamin Franklin in Hungary." *Hungarian Studies in English* 10 (1976): 12-13.

Morris, Richard B. *The Peacemakers: The Great Powers and American Independence*. New York: Harper and Row, 1965.

Pace, Antonio. *Benjamin Franklin and Italy*. Philadelphia: American Philosophical Society, 1958.

Roider, Karl. "William Lee–Our First Envoy in Vienna." *Virginia Magazine of History and Biography* 86.2 (Apr. 1978): 163-68.

Schlitter, Hanns. *Die Beziehung Österreichs zu Amerika.* Innsbruck: Verlag der Wagner'schen Universitäts-Buchhandlung, 1885.

Schwartz, Thomas. "Roundtable Review: Introduction." *SHAFR Passport* 45.1 (April, 2014): 6-15.

Zaker, Ernst-Victor. *Geschichte der Wiener Journalisten von den Anfängen bis zum Jahre 1848*. Vienna, 1892.

THE IRONY OF FREUD AND THE AMERICANS: WHAT LIES BENEATH THE SURFACE

JEANNE C. HOLLAND

INTRODUCTION

Sigmund Freud's system of ideas that he labeled "psychoanalysis" in 1895 was warmly received in America, particularly in New England between 1900 and 1915, at the same time that it was extensively rejected in Europe as the "Jewish Science." The conventional, and often scholarly, explanation for Freud's popularity in the United States rests on the perception that this Austrian neurologist was the enemy of American Puritanism because he openly addressed sexual issues that were long avoided by the Victorians of his age. In this context, Freud is perceived as optimistic and liberating. However, the Americans who welcomed psychoanalysis as a serious science saw in it the dark remnants of their Calvinist heritage, rather than a novel or superficial gimmick to discuss sex. The most important proponents of Freud's early ideas were G. Stanley Hall, first President of Clark University, and James Jackson Putnam, an admired Harvard neurologist. Freud's "discovery" (as he put it) resonated with both men because it revealed the murky contours of the psyche's inner landscape. Both Hall and Putnam were direct biological descendants of their American Calvinist forebears, and they were drawn to Freud's "Id Psychology" because of their understanding of the complexities of the psyche.

Freud's struggle in Europe to be accepted was signaled in his correspondence with, as Freud declared, his "son and heir" Carl Jung. He wrote, "Germany probably won't take any notice of psychoanalysis until some bigwig has solemnly recognized it." He sarcastically added that the quickest way would be to "attract the interest of Kaiser Wilhelm, who is known to understand everything" (Jones II: 37). The United States provided Freud with the "big wigs" he needed to present and promote his ideas. Until his death in 1939, he graciously welcomed the academic contributions of a few Americans. However, he often disapproved of American customs and beliefs, and his attitudes concerning the New World were characterized by a deep ambivalence. His sincere regard for some individuals, coupled with his urge to have his theories accepted quickly, provided the impetus for his few favorable impressions. However, over the years as deviations from psychoanalysis led to what Freud labeled "abuses," he became increasingly hostile toward American culture.

Without any appreciation for Hall's and Putnam's intellectual Calvinist roots, Freud was flattered by his welcome into the American intellectual community of the early 1900s. But he was baffled by the warm welcome his view of human nature received. He commented that American intellectual culture (if there even was such a thing) showed an "absence of any deep-rooted scientific tradition…and the much less stringent rule of official authority" (S. Freud, *Works* XIV: 32) that characterized European practice and custom. He thought of Americans as naive and hungry for the novel, rather than sophisticated enough to accept his dark grasp understanding of the psyche. By 1900, Europe had largely rejected psychoanalysis because of its sexual content, "bizarre" support of infant sexuality and its Jewish roots. However, Freud's construct of the human mind as complicated and shadowy, with its deepest recesses inaccessible to most people, aligned almost perfectly with the great Calvinist minds of the early American intellectual tradition. These minds included Cotton Mather and Jonathan Edwards. Therefore, when Hall and Putnam, the neo-Puritan progeny of the American Calvinists, read Freud's early work published in *Imago* and the *Jahrbuch,* they recognized a moral perspective that beckoned directly back to their own Calvinist heritage.

G. STANLEY HALL AND JAMES JACKSON PUTNAM

G. Stanley Hall, the father of American psychology, and the famous Harvard neurologist James Jackson Putnam were early and dedicated enthusiasts of Freud's Id Psychology. Id Psychology provided the foundation for Freud's later development of the Ego and the Superego. Both Hall and Putnam were born and reared in Protestant homes in Massachusetts. They shared the Puritan intellectual heritage woven through the curriculum at Harvard University. In addition, Hall studied religion at Union Theological Seminary in New York to become a clergyman. In Hall's boyhood, the Congregationalist Church was the religious and social center for the community. The more moderate Congregational Church derived its basic theology from the older Calvinist institutions of Hall's forbears.

Hall's New England heritage began with the arrivals of William Bradford and John Winthrop. Bradford established the Plymouth Plantation in Massachusetts in 1620, and Winthrop established the Massachusetts Bay Company in 1630 sermonizing that "We must consider that we shall be as a city upon a Hill" (36). Both Bradford and Winthrop left England to pursue their unrestrained devotion to Calvinism, as instructed by John Calvin in his *Institutes of the Christian Religion.* The Church of England was far too "impure" for its doctrine to hold any meaning for these "Puritans," whose job it was to "purify" it from the apostasy of Rome and other negative influences. In his *Life and Confessions of a Psychologist*, Hall explained his family tree as it related to the early Puritans:

> On my mother's side, my great-great grandmother was Abigail Alden, a direct descendant in the fifth generation of John Alden (b. 1599) of Plymouth fame [and] on my father's side we trace the name Hall through nine generations to John Hall who at twenty-one came from Coventry, England, to Charleston, Massachusetts, in 1630, in the fleet with Governor Winthrop. (22)

In his *Confessions*, Hall described explicit sexual behaviors he encountered at grammar school that would make his Victorian contemporaries blush but would also be understood by Calvinist and Freudian alike. He recited a list of "rotten" behaviors including "homosexuality, exhibitionism, fellatio, onanism, relations with animals, and every form of perversion" (133). With his clear-eyed recollection of boyhood sexual behavior, Hall was well prepared for Freud's revelations about the Id and its sexual secrets.

G. Stanley Hall, Clark University's first president (1889-1920) surprised Freud by unreservedly supporting many of his innovations. So taken was Hall with the aspects of Id Psychology that he invited Freud and his associate Carl Jung to speak at the celebration of Clark University's twentieth anniversary in 1909 (Jones II: 60). Freud accepted, and upon his return to Austria, he wrote to his Swiss friend Oskar Pfister, "Who could have known that over there in America, only an hour away from Boston, there was a respectable old gentleman waiting impatiently for the next number of the *Jahrbuch* reading and understanding it all" (E. Freud, *Letters* 22).

Although Hall's moral values were grounded in Calvinism, his intellectual interests were concentrated in the natural science and philosophy of the nineteenth century. As he extended his education beyond the religious curriculum of Union Theological Seminary, he noted, "Had I not set out from so narrow and saturated an orthodoxy my sense of progress would have been far less" (184). In 1868, he arrived in Bonn, Germany to expand his studies to include "Darwin, Spencer, Tyndall, Renan, Strauss, Emerson and Carlyle," and he acknowledged the influence of "Coleridge, Feuerbach, Comte, Schwegler, Hagenbach, Theodore Parker, Tom Paine, Lessing and Goethe" (185). From his reading, he added the intellectual riches of his age to his Puritan heritage. He became fluent in German, so his reading of Freud was nuanced and sophisticated. In spite of Hall's progressive interests, his parents hoped that Hall would become a clergyman. Ironically, it was the famous American preacher, Henry Ward Beecher, who funded Hall's studies in Europe. Ultimately, Hall studied neurology and the new field of psychology under William James at Harvard. Because he had combined religious studies with his intellectual activities, he was not only able to understand Freud's system of psychoanalysis, but found it resonated with him in a way that was almost spiritual.

Hall was one of the first American psychologists to take an interest in the theories of Freud. In his *Confessions*, Hall commented that he had "long been predisposed to certain special interests in sex psychology besides those which every human being has had since man became man" (406). Recalling his own youthful sexual misadventures, he explained, "Perhaps my prepubescent observations [...] opened my eyes to the possibilities of precocious evil in this field" (406). Hall held a view of children that was closer to the Puritan image of "innocent vipers" than the Romantic picture of innocence. In this way, his views were compatible with Freud's "discoveries" about infant and childhood sexuality. By inviting the Viennese neurologist to speak, Hall facilitated the introduction of Freudian ideas to many Americans. Through Hall's imprimatur, prominent members of the American intellectual and medical community first embraced these ideas.

Hall's efforts to bring psychoanalysis to the United States were intensified by James Jackson Putnam, Professor of Neuropathology at Harvard. Putnam proved to be an amenable convert to many of Freud's tenets, and his stature in Boston society and its medical community pleased his European mentor very much. Understanding his good fortune in attracting the interest and goodwill of this Boston Brahmin, Freud was delighted to gain his support for the "cause." In 1906, Putnam published the first paper in English to discuss Freudian methods in the *Journal of Abnormal Psychology*. Thus, his interest in this subject preceded his introduction to Freud by several years.

Upon meeting in 1909, they established a relationship that would last until Professor Putnam's death in 1918. The two friends corresponded frequently, often in German, sharing philosophies as well as personal histories. After Putnam's death, Freud eulogized him as the American who was

> [a]ble to do perhaps more than anyone for the spread of psycho-analysis in his own country, [protecting] it from aspersions which, on the other side of the Atlantic no less than this, inevitably have been cast upon it. But all such reproaches were bound to be silenced when a man of Putnam's lofty ethical standards and moral rectitude had ranked himself among the supporters of the new science and of the therapeutics based upon it. (*Preface* 269)

Like Hall, Putnam traced his roots back to New England Calvinists. Using his maternal grandfather's memoir, he traced his family's Calvinist heritage to the founding of the Massachusetts Bay Colony where his ancestor Edward Jackson settled in 1643 in Cambridge. Edward Jackson helped to expand Harvard College as the Puritan institution to educate the colony's young men. Dying in 1681, he left a comfortable estate to his son Jonathan who, like his father, was a staunch Calvinist and a prominent member of the community. Putnam himself was born in Boston in 1846. His parents had exchanged the stricter Calvinist-based Congregationalism for a more liberal brand of Puritanism, and reared him as a Unitarian. He graduated from Harvard at the age of twenty in 1866 and immediately entered Harvard Medical School. Putnam was from an elite Boston medical family. His father specialized in obstetrics and women's diseases, and his grandfather James Jackson enjoyed the reputation of being the city's premier physician, who helped to found Massachusetts General Hospital. Neurology attracted Putnam because he was interested in the brain and nervous system as well as the diseases that affected these organs. At Harvard, he established a permanent friendship with William James, one of his classmates, and upon completing his studies in 1869, Putnam went to Germany where he added electrotherapeutics to his neurological background.

In 1870, neurology was a relatively new field in which the brain was considered the organ of the mind. Certain organic conditions such as an injury to brain tissue, a lesion with the brain, or a disease like syphilis were thought to precipitate affective states, and the cure involved operations or drugs. *Materia medica* was, however, undermined when certain neurologists began to investigate the role psychological states played in precipitating physical illnesses. With these new theories, causation was reversed from the physical to the mental or emotional. In Europe, Putnam studied with two neurologists—Theodore Meynert in Vienna and Jean Charcot in Paris. Meynert was Freud's mentor at the University of Vienna. Over a decade later, Freud unwittingly followed Putnam's path as he, too, studied with these specialists.

Fluent in German and familiar with the latest neurological findings, Putnam returned to Boston in 1872 to join the Harvard medical faculty. For many years, he continued to believe that nervous ailments were caused by organic brain dysfunction. Using this material basis, he had hoped to find a link between damaged brain tissue and emotional symptoms, but his investigations yielded nothing that would shed light on this connection. Slowly he began to defect from the strict materialism of organic causation as he became willing to consider that within the mind certain psychological states produce physical symptoms. This in turn led him openly to consider the viability of mental therapeutics. In this interest, he joined Josiah Royce, Hugo Munsterberg, and his old friend William James who, together, formed the Boston "school." They "developed the most sophisticated and scientific psychotherapy in the English-speaking world" (Hale 75). As a group, these men met regularly between 1890 and 1909, the year of Freud's visit. The Boston "school" owed no debt to Freud for its therapeutics. In fact, in 1906 Putnam believed that Freud would be remembered primarily for extending the theories of Pierre Janet rather than for contributing something original to medicine.

However, becoming familiar with Freud's "talking cure," Putnam found this non-invasive approach an attractive method by which to treat some patients' nervous complaints. After Putnam met Freud at Clark University, the two men discovered that they shared a common medical background, which became the foundation for their personal friendship. Their relationship was marked by a moral earnestness on the part of Putnam and a political shrewdness on the part of Freud. However, his evaluation of Putnam as a "magnificent acquisition" for the "cause" was always tempered by warmth (E. Freud 76). Putnam thanked Freud for reinstating a complicated view of the psyche. In defense of Freud's provocative focus on dark sexual mysteries, Putnam pointed out that although the "detective novel is welcome at every fireside [...] the scientific student of the human acts and motives is considered a disseminator of morbid tendencies" (Putnam 1921: 78).

Putnam criticized the idealism of his age that produced the Emersonian "sky blue optimism" denounced by William James. America was in the grip of new religious doctrine of Methodist Perfectionism. This doctrine heralded a new age in which people could perfect themselves through spiritual development. Perfectionism was the human ally of the New Republic's confidence in "Manifest Destiny." It sought its roots in the *New Testament* passage that allowed for the individual to "Be Ye therefore perfect, even as your Father in Heaven in perfect" (Matthew 5:58). In a peculiar American application of this command, all good things could come to individuals and the nation through the optimism that God blessed America. America's earliest religious and intellectual tradition of Calvinism was turned upside down by the sanguinity of nineteenth-century Emersonian idealism that claimed one could become perfect.

FREUD'S ID PSYCHOLOGY REVITALIZES AMERICAN CALVINISM

In 1909, Freud delivered in German five lectures at Clark University. The content of these lectures included Freud's "discovery" about infant sexuality that he described as "polymorphous perverse." With the opening of this Pandora's Box, Freud unleashed the old Calvinist view of children as "innocent vipers." In this doctrine, children came into this world carrying the stain of original sin. Within the Calvinist introspective tradition the best outcome for enduring, but not eliminating, this sin was to inspect the darkest corners of the human heart. Then through confession, or talking, people could be somewhat relieved of their psychic burdens caused by the original sin of Adam and Eve. Cotton Mather (1663-1728), one of America's most prominent Calvinist Divines, consistently linked troubled psychic states to somatic illnesses. As we have seen, with the advent of neurology that looked to the physical to explain the mental, nineteenth-century medicine reversed the earlier view of psychosomatic illness strongly held by Cotton Mather and further articulated by Jonathan Edwards (1703-1758), two of America's most influential men of religion, theologians and philosophers alike.

Having been reared a Unitarian, Putnam rationally rejected the doctrine of original sin, which he believed negatively colored the Calvinism of his ancestors. Therefore, when he mentioned the similarity between this doctrine and Freud's theories on infant sexuality in his 1915 work *Human Motives*,

Putnam sought to clarify his own position and disconnect from his ancestral Doctrine of Original Sin: "If anyone should imagine that it was my intention to characterize the period of infancy and childhood as one of gross sensuality—of such a sort, for example, as really to justify in a psychological sense the term 'original sin,' […] they would be very much mistaken" (81). In a stunning contradiction, however, Putnam almost immediately slipped into a description of native depravity, i.e. Original Sin: "A striking fact about the infant is that he comes into the world as the inheritor of tendencies which had their original and usefulness in the dark period of his development" (82).

In his recognition of the contradictions within the normal psyche, we see Putnam's effort to balance the idealism of his age with Freudian realism that harkened back to the gritty realism of Calvinism. Emersonian idealism eschewed introspection as a futile exercise that was at odds with the progress of perfectionism. Rejecting the perfectionist notion that "introspection is of the devil," Putnam argued that this belief would naively "press constantly forward into…more abundant light…[forgetting] those who have had a dark history." He added that it is the "narrow intolerance to cry 'introspection' in an effort to prevent an unfortunate invalid…from searching, even to the death, causes of his misery" (1921: 79-80). In his acceptance of people's inherently evil tendencies, Putnam's views were at odds with the conventional wisdom of his era, which stressed individual perfectibility. If psychoanalysis were a religious doctrine, perfectibility would be considered heresy. The most that Calvinist and Freudian could hope for was amelioration or improvement, but never perfection.

In 1911 at the Psycho-Analytic Congress held in Weimar, Putnam delivered his "Plea for the Study of Philosophic Methods in Preparation of Psychoanalytic Work." In this "Plea" Putnam stated, "The main service of the psychoanalytic investigations which have been made so far, under the impulse of Freud's genius, has been that of forcing us to recognize the repressed devils that lurk within us" (1921: 89). Freud often used the image of devils to illuminate psychic states. However, unlike Freud, Putnam feared "the deterministic world to which natural science" pointed. Not entirely abandoning the optimistic spirit of his American culture, he contended that within the unconscious mind more can be found than just the "shady side of human nature." He argued, "The mind itself contains a real, permanently abiding element […] of which the life of the universe, itself is made." He concluded that if a scientific system fails to recognize the "world of the spirit," then it could not, in and of itself, explain everything about the personality" (1921: 90-91). These pronouncements about the positive side of human nature held him back from going over the cliff of Freudian determinism. By introducing the human spirit as an affirmative force, Putnam had merged the hopefulness of perfectionism with the Calvinism's darkness of the psyche.

Attending the Congress, Freud listened respectfully to his American friend's attempt to infuse the unseen Spirit into the scientific system of psychoanalysis. When Putnam finished, Freud commented to his colleague Ernest Jones that the "Plea" reminded him of a lovely "centerpiece" that receives admiration but no serious attention (Jones III: 86). In the introduction that Freud wrote to Putnam's *Addresses on Psycho-Analysis* in 1921, he described the mind of this Bostonian as "pre-eminently ethical and philosophical." Nevertheless, Freud was never sympathetic to Putnam's attempts to dress psychoanalysis in quasi-theological clothing. In spite of Putnam's desire to apply psychoanalysis as a spiritual remedy to heal the sick soul, he remained dependent upon Freud's mental map grounded in the Id and excluding any spiritual realm. Reared in the atmosphere of moral perfectionism, Putnam never openly rejected this heritage. But he did long for a more profound view of the human condition than that which was embodied within Emersonian idealism. Freud's ideas, therefore, provided Putnam with the "scientific" principles that allowed him to re-enter the "dark woods" to encounter the "imps of darkness" expressed in the Calvinism of his forebears.

Psychoanalysis revitalized certain neglected aspects of the human experience after Calvinism's decline, and Putnam seized upon Freud's "discoveries" of the unconscious mind to help heal the wounded psyche. True to his American religious heritage of Calvinism and Emersonian perfectionism, Putnam sought to elevate psychoanalysis to a metaphysical system, and himself concluded that Freud was a "courageous, unflinching, pioneer-investigator and a man of genius [but] as a philosopher he is weak" (1921: 116).

In many respects, the American Puritans and Sigmund Freud shared a common mental terrain shaped by the following features: an emphasis on people's concupiscent, sexual natures; an Old Testament or Hebraic heritage which underscored the strength of the affections; a deterministic explanation of the innate capacity for iniquity in all individuals, even children; a belief in introspection as the way to reveal the twists in character; and an effort to restrain the irrational forces within a person's mind through reason. Not appreciating how closely his view of human nature corresponded to

Calvinism, Freud explained that Americans accepted his ideas because they lacked any kind of intellectual heritage that could be summoned to challenge his "discoveries" as they had been challenged and rejected by many in his native Europe.

So when Freud came to Massachusetts bearing his gifts of infant sexuality, innate urges, and unruly affections, many of the men and women in the audience were prepared for him because they were at least familiar with the moral concerns of their ancestors: American Calvinists. Freud revitalized a cultural legacy that lay buried beneath the optimism of the nineteenth century. Deep chords were struck as he described the human psyche as the battleground in which the fragile forces of reason were pitted against the potent energies of irrationality. The cure, Freud, announced, for this psychic chaos was as old as the hills: introspection followed by confession, two exercises that were at the heart of the Puritan experience. William James, who was in the audience at Clark University, declared, "'The future of psychology belongs to […] Freud's work,' as the past belonged to the Calvinists" (Hale 18).

AMERICAN CALVINISTS' VIEW OF HUMAN NATURE: COTTON MATHER AND JONATHAN EDWARDS

Within the American Puritan communicants of the seventeenth and eighteenth centuries, evil motives were ascribed to Original Sin, something that each individual inherited from the first miscreants, Adam and Eve. Because these early colonists accepted that all persons, even infants, were naturally depraved and therefore filled with wickedness, they were very open about their personal inclinations toward sin, including sexual misbehavior. To them, human nature seemed to be shaped by forces beyond the individual's control. Therefore, restraint of one's lower nature was not easily achieved, though always set as the goal. In spite of this deterministic view, they insisted that it was everyone's duty to God to try to master corrupt impulses before they inflicted damage on oneself and others. The Puritans saw sex within bounds as something good and positive. As Freud did later, they distinguished between obsessive, selfish desires and the restrained enjoyment of earthly pleasures. It was not the Puritans who repressed sex but the Victorians of Freud's age.

Cotton Mather's View of Affective States Causing Physical Illness

Within the American intellectual experience, long before the advent of Freudianism and neo-Freudianism, Puritans spoke and wrote about the unruly affections that lurk beneath the thin veneer of reason. The colonials who preceded Freud by almost two centuries possessed certain insights that may seem far-sighted to us today in our post-Freudian world, but in fact came from a view of the human condition infected with Original Sin or pre-determined instincts. This sin could be met with introspection, confession and reason—Puritan and Freudian virtues alike. The great Puritan Divine Cotton Mather expressed his "cure" for mental disease as follows: "*Diseases* that seem *Incurable*, are easily cure by *Conversation* [...] And as long as the *Passions of the Mind* continue, the *Diseases* may indeed change their *Forms*; but they rarely quitt the Patients" (1972: 43). Mather holds a unique place in American history and letters because of the role he played in shaping the consciousness of the incipient New England culture. The sheer heft of his writings and his diversity of topics are rivaled by Freud and other prolific writers. Both men generated several hundred texts during their lifetimes and by publishing their ideas they influenced their generation and established an intellectual legacy to which future generations are heirs.

In his sermons, journals and treatises, Mather expressed a fascination with what we call human psychology, although no such expression existed in the seventeenth century. Possessing an intensely curious nature, he explored the relationship between the mind and body, establishing a connection, which anticipated the field of psychosomatic medicine, which only gained legitimacy with the investigations of Freud. Mather suggested what Freud "discovered" several hundred years later—that "passions" are at the root of many illnesses, including forms of hysteria, and that the mind and body are linked in such a way that one affects the other. In a tone that foreshadowed our contemporary cynicism about medical doctors, Mather also recognized how little physicians of his day really knew about the etiology of illness: "*Physicians* talk about the *Causes* of *Diseases*. But their Talk is very *conjectural*, very *uncertain*, very *ambiguous*; and oftentimes a mere *Jargon*; and in it, they are full of *contradiction* to one another" (1972: 43).

Mather's reputation suffered because of his presumed involvement in the Salem witch trials of 1693. He did not participate as a judge in the trials, but did agree to write an account of the trials: *The Wonders of the Unseen World*. Perry Miller, American historian, called this "A false book, produced by a man whose heart was not in it" (Mather 1977: 12). But it served to unite irrevocably the name of Cotton Mather to one of the grimmest episodes in New England's history. However, Mather was not a gloomy conservative; instead, in several important areas he exhibited liberal tendencies. He was very much impressed with scientific innovations, including spectacles for the eyes and an improved compass. Believing that these improvements came from God, he was often on the frontier of scientific discovery. His interest in his daughters' training was particularly striking because he wanted them to be educated according to their inclinations, including medicine. He even regretted that his own beloved ministry was closed to them.

In his sermons, Mather demonstrated a profoundly modern understanding of human psychology, in which he discerned tendencies that are more often ascribed to Freud than to an American divine. Frequently employing descriptions of physical diseases as analogies for psychological states, Mather in one rousing sermon that must surely have gained the attention of even the most apathetic souls, declared that each "has the palsey of an unsteady mind;...the Feavour of unchastity...the Cancer of Envy;...the Tympany of Pride." Taking a final measure of his parishioners, he demanded to know, "Where am I preaching, Sirs, but in a Hospital?" (1700: 3). Like Freud, he described human nature as essentially fixed, or determined. People can no more change than can leopards change their spots. Accepting that humanity is attracted to the perverse, he explained, "People find rather pleasure than trouble in most horrible customes....If we are accustomed unto any thing, we naturally crave after it." He added his view that emotions are essentially recalcitrant when he wrote that "we don't care to break a custome; tis a strain upon our nature to do so" (1965: 184).

For Mather, and later Freud, the only hope of improvement comes from seeking within oneself a higher knowledge of personal motivation, a process that Mather explained "would be richly worth the while, for us and everyone to examine himself" (1965: 197). He was willing to take his own psychological medicine when he wrote, "It is herewithal my Resolution also, to keep a watchful Eye on all my Sinful Inclinations; and Suppress and Subdue still in all their tendencies" (1952, II: 18). Throughout his life, Mather's view of the human condition remained essentially pessimistic as he complained, "The most of men lead bad lives" (1952, II: 341). In his *Diary*, he lamented his habit of masturbating and acknowledged that is caused him great grief throughout his life. Because he understood the impact of sexual tension on one's soma, he cried that he would "recover a wondrous Degree of Heath, if…[he] were not broken by the Distresses, & Grievous Temptations" (1952, I: 467). He referred to the sexual instincts as "special soul-harassing point[s]," "grievous Distresses," "great vexations," "Temptations of Clamour" and "sorrowful Directresses" (1952, I: 467-90 *passim*). Not until the advent of Freudian theory did sexual instincts again receive so much attention for being at the root of human suffering. Within his own psyche, Mather made a strong connection between repressed erotic impulses and ill health. Freud later affirmed Mather's understanding of repressed desires as the most prevalent cause of hysteria.

Commenting that one-third of all diseases are "chronical," Mather said that of this one-third, one-half are forms of hysteria. He wrote: "It is marvellous to see, in how many forms we undergo *Splenetic* and *Hysteric* Maladies; the very Toothache itself often belongs to them" (1972: 36). He believed that the cure for hysteria is "conversation," a method Freud also propounded after he experienced some remarkable recoveries because of the "talking cure" (S. Freud, XI: 13). Mather suggested, "Lett the *Physician* with all possible Ingenuity of *conversation*, find out, what matter of anxiety there may have been upon the mind of the *Patient*." Once the "*Burden*" has been discovered, then "Lett him use all the ways he can to take it off" (1972: 138). He recognized that hysteria often results from disturbed thoughts, and the most effective method for improvement was the patient's ability to recognize and describe certain affective states.

Whereas Mather's writings on hysteria was unknown to Freud (in his writings, Freud never mentioned Mather nor Edwards), one of Freud's early patients was Frau Emmy von N., whom he described in *Studies on Hysteria* as having "storms in her head," which resulted in partial paralysis (S. Freud, II: 8). While treating her, he first determined that repression causes "the inaccessibility to fresh associations of a group of ideas…with one of the extremities of the body" (S. Freud, II: 86). This repression was experienced as the loss of memory regarding a certain experience that precipitated the hysterical symptoms. Freud believed that it was his task to help restore his patient's memory so that she could confront her suppressed impulses, regardless of their nature, which he believed were sexual. In a similar vein, Mather previously cited faulty memory as the cause of paralysis when he suggested that "Paralyticks" need to be reminded of "their sins, which…may be, too much forgotten." Once "Paralyticks" face the sins in their hearts, then they can be restored to sensibility. He believed that people unconsciously become paralyzed (with hysteria) as a result of their degenerate thoughts. And demonstrating the causal relationship for which Freud would later become famous, he explained that people unknowingly deaden a certain part, or parts of their body, because this is the only way they can prevent themselves "from committing [an] abundance of actual sins" (1972: 138). In this condition, human beings "are under a necessity of Living so *Unactively*, that they may perhaps think themselves to live almost *Innocently*" (1972: 138).

According to Mather, the bright side to immobility was that "a Paralytick Distemper, does restrain People from committing…sins" (1972: 138). Freud believed that certain neuroses constrain the individual who might otherwise have acted on these darker impulses, and he suggested that the inhibitions caused by the Oedipal conflict provide just such curbs on youthful sexual passion. Both Mather and Freud agreed that people cause their own paralyzed conditions because in this state their aggressive instincts are inhibited. They further acknowledged that once people became victims of their own hysteria, they would forget their "former sins," or thoughts, that led to their disabilities.

Mather often linked madness to melancholia, and in his discussion of this bleak emotional state he exhibited a sensitivity that was, perhaps, from personal experience. He insisted that people who suffer from the condition should not be scolded because they "sufficiently *Afflict themselves*," and become "their own *Tormentors*." Understanding the delusions of the sufferers, he wrote that "they create a world of *Imaginary Ones* [troubles], and by *Meditating Terror*, they make themselves as miserable, as they could be from the most *Real Miseries*" (1972: 133). His solution anticipated the methods of psychoanalysis when he suggested that instead of trying to brighten the sufferer's mood, the physician should listen carefully to the "tedious *Way* of [their] *complaining against themselves*" and to "allow that all their *Complaints* may be True" (1972: 134). Mather continued that if you "trace" the melancholiacs' troubles back to some cause, "You may perhaps find out, that some very intolerable *Vexation* […] began their Uneasiness, and first raised that Ulcer in their minds, which now finds *New Matter* to work upon, and the *Old Matter* is not Longer Spoken of. Mather's notions of "old matter" and "new matter" anticipated Freud's theory of repression in which original disturbing memories are buried and replaced by "screen memoires," which are more tolerable (1972: 134). The "screen memory" acts as a blind that is drawn over the unhappy recollection. Describing a process that Freud later labeled "transference," Mather noticed that "Cured melancholiacs hate their doctors and all others concerned with their illness and recovery" (1972:

135). Had Freud read Mather, he might have laughed at Mather's profound insight that the cured tend to hate the curer. During the cure, however, patients are dependent on their healers and can develop an unhealthy admiration through the transference of affections.

The Talking Cure and Parricides All

Cotton Mather and Sigmund Freud both believed that healing occurred, in many cases, through revealing one's "vexations" and troubling thoughts to Puritan divines or psychoanalysts. "Talking" was the simple treatment that would undercover profound disturbances in the psyche. Both men considered trusted that their "patients" could gain insights necessary to participate in their recovery of spiritual/emotional health. Both men treated women through "talking" as the only approach to their patients illnesses. Cotton Mather had Martha Goodwin and Freud had Anna O. Anna O. was actually Josef Breuer's patient, but it was through Breuer's sharing his work with Freud that both neurologists understood the power of talking, or "confession."

In 1693, Martha Goodwin lived with the Mathers after her traumatic experiences as a witness to, and perhaps a victim of or a participant in, "witchcraft" in Salem that year. Mather believed Martha had been affectively damaged by her experiences, and he treated her for "demonological possession" while she lived in his home. His cure was to listen carefully to all of her complaints. He encouraged her to talk about her "possession," and he expressed compassion toward this young girl. Instead of being rescued and treated by Mather, Martha Goodwin could have been pressed or stoned to death—the fate of others who were connected to the Salem witch trials.

In *Wonders of the Unseen World*, Mather described Martha's symptoms as follows: she was unable to eat; her mouth would become paralyzed; her vision was blurry and at times she was blind when she tried to read the Bible; she had a permanent cough; and she hung her head as if her neck were broken (*passim*). Eventually, through talking and confessing, Martha recovered her emotional health. Similarly, to his audience at Clark University, Freud described the now famous patient Anna O. in these terms: she experienced rigid paralysis, weight loss, blurred vision, and difficulties with keeping her head up. She had a persistent nervous cough, reduced powers of speech, and was subject to delirium and the alteration of her whole personality. Josef Breuer and Sigmund Freud in *Studies in Hysteria* (1895) published Anna

O.'s story. To many, her case marks the beginning of psychoanalysis because Breuer treated Anna entirely through talk. Anna O. herself dubbed her improvement the "Talking Cure." Although Freud and Breuer were oblivious to Martha Goodwin's "cure" through confession and talking, people in his audience at Clark were familiar with the Salem witch trials (1693) and knew, however vaguely, of the great Puritan Divine, Cotton Mather. So two hundred years earlier in Boston, Massachusetts, Cotton Mather treated Martha Goodwin in ways remarkably similar to the way Anna O. was treated in the late 1800s in Vienna.

In addition to the Calvinist echoes in the "Talking Cure," Freud wrote about the Oedipal instincts in young boys. In *Totem and Taboo* (1909), Freud suggested that boys want to kill their fathers to eliminate competition, at first with the mother but ultimately to be the Über-male in the family. In his study of a five-year old boy, Freud reports that the child

> [r]egarded his father (as he made all too clear) as a competitor for the favours of his mother, towards whom the obscure foreshadowings of his budding sexual wishes were aimed. Thus he was situated in the typical attitude of a male child towards his parents to which we have given the name of the 'Œdipus complex' and which we regard in general as the nuclear complex of the neuroses. (S. Freud, XIII: 150)

Long before Freud's theory about fathers and sons, another great Puritan Divine, Jonathan Edwards, made clear in his ferocious sermon, *Men Naturally the Enemies of God,* that there is competition between Creator and creature. Edwards described the same aggressive instinct Freud later discerned in the sons who killed the "primal father" in *Totem and Taboo.* Freud's mythic tribal murder set men free from the father's powerful authority. Seeking autonomy from stern authority was a motive that Edwards anticipated when he explained that people would kill God if they could because His death would set them "at liberty" from his "strict law." Once freed from God's discipline, a person might say, "I take my liberty to walk in the way I like best and not be continually in such a slavish fear of God's Displeasure" (VII: 180).

Edwards believed that whereas people seek their independence from their Maker, they also lack the insight to understand their shadowy temptations. They barely glimpse their hatred when they whine, "God has not done well by me in many instances....He has shown mercy to others, and refused it to me" (VII: 176). Admonishing his congregations that "indeed natural men cannot kill God," and therefore "make no attempts," he explained that lack of action is "no argument that this is not the tendency of the principle (VII: 180). Understanding that many of the people to whom he was speaking could not possibly conceive of themselves as parricides, he interpreted their resistance:

> Some natural men may be ready to say, I do not know that I feel any such enmity in my heart against God as is spoke of....If I have such enmity, why do not I feel it? [...]. How can others see what is in my heart better than I myself? [....] If I hate one of my fellow creatures, and have a spirit against him, I can feel it inwardly working. (VII: 175)

But Edwards does not accept that a lack of self-awareness is a sufficient test of purity of heart. He explained that "[i]f you but observe yourself, and search your own heart, unless you are strangely blinded, you may be sensible of these things where in enmity does fundamentally consist" (VII: 176). So it is not an innocent spirit that restrains people, but their "having always been taught that God is infinitely above" them (VII: 180). He believed that "the heart is like a viper, hissing, and spiting...at God...and however free from it the heart may seem to be when let alone and secure...a change of circumstances will bring out that which was hid before" (VII: 165).

One cannot help but imagine that Freud would be delighted with Edward's graphic image of the heart. Throughout his life, Freud remained a secular Jew and an atheist. However, many of his views on the desperation of the human condition coincided with religious views on the fallen state of men and women. Whereas God was the ultimate Father to Jonathan Edwards, the human father was the ultimate authority to Freud. Like Edwards, Freud believed that people wanted to kill the authority for personal gain, and he found his example in *Oedipus Rex.*

CONCLUSION

When G. Stanley Hall and James Jackson Putnam encountered Freud's ideas at the beginning of the twentieth century, they found themselves irresistibly attracted to certain elements of psychoanalysis. These included the unconscious mind, innate depravity, the role of the affections in causing illness and the sublimation of instincts. Hall and Putnam were familiar with their Calvinist heritage, which had predisposed them to accept the reality of these concepts. However, they did not treat them as religious notions; instead, they claimed them in the name of science. By replacing the doctrine of Original Sin with the instincts of the Id, they accepted Freud's discovery of psychoanalysis in the spirit of advancement in the American age of progress.

It was fortuitous for Freud that Hall and Putnam were fluent in German. Particularly in Hall's case, his fluency allowed him to become acquainted with Freud's early ideas at the end of the nineteenth century. His regard for Freud's "discoveries" led him to invite the Austrian neurologist to Clark University. It was during this visit that Freud received the only honorary doctorate he was to get during his life. Working with Freud's ideas, Hall and Putnam paved the way for the establishment of psychoanalysis in America. Although Freud never appreciated the background of the reasons that his ideas received such an enthusiastic greeting in this country, his unfamiliarity with the New England intellectual tradition does not cancel its influence. When Freud visited New England in 1909, he arrived in a region were social and psychological perspectives were rooted in the soil of self-scrutiny and confession. To the influential New Englanders who listened to him, his theories were considered to be liberating precisely because he did not present them as religious doctrine, but offered them instead as the fruits of scientific discovery.

During his brief three-week visit to New England, Freud remained evidently unaware of America's Calvinist roots, which caused psychoanalysis to flourish. Using the language of the laboratory, Freud restated the Puritan conviction that at heart people are dominated by unconscious aggressive and self-serving instincts—a view largely eclipsed during the nineteenth century by Methodist perfectionism and Emersonian idealism. Even though Freud was not aware of the similarities between his system of ideas and those of American Calvinists, certain American intellectuals recognized the common features of human nature in both approaches to the psyche. In many respects, neither Calvinist nor Freudian views of human nature were characterized by optimism, in that both considered people lacked the ability to overcome the dark tendencies of their own unregenerate temperaments. It fell to ministers and psychoanalysts, respectively, to uncover the repressed emotions that caused illness.

WORKS CITED

Edwards, Jonathan. *The Works of Jonathan Edwards.* 7 vol. Ed. Perry Miller. New Haven: Yale UP, 1957.

Freud, Ernest. *Letters of Sigmund Freud.* New York: Basic Books, 1960.

Freud, Sigmund. "On the History of the Psychoanalytic Movement." 1914. *The Standard Edition of the Complete Psychological Works of Sigmund Freud*. 24 vol. Ed. James Strachey. London: Hogarth P, 1953-1974.

—. "Preface to J.J. Putnam's 'Addresses on Psycho-analysis.'" *Standard Edition*. 18 vol.

Hale, Nathan G. *James Jackson Putnam and Psychoanalysis: Correspondence with Sigmund Freud, William James, Ernest Jones, Morton Prince and Sandor Ferenczi.* Cambridge, MA: Harvard UP, 1971.

Hall, G. Stanley. *Life and Confessions of a Psychologist*. New York: D. Appleton and Co., 1923.

Jones, Ernest. *Sigmund Freud: Life and Works*. 3 vol. London: Hogarth P, 1953-1955.

Mather, Cotton. *Advice from the Watch Tower: A Faithful Testimony Against Evil Customes*. 1691. New York: Frederick Ungar Publishing Co., 1965.

—. *The Angel of Bethesda*. 1721. Barre, MA.: American Antiquarian Society and Barre Publishers, 1972.

—. *Diary of Cotton Mather.* 1691. 2 vol. New York: Frederick Ungar Publishing Co., 1952.

—. *Magnalia Christi Americana*. 1702. 2 vol. Cambridge, MA.: Harvard UP, 1977.

—. *The Great Physician*. Boston: Timothy Green's P, 1700.

—. *Wonders of the Unseen World.* 1693. New York: Frederick Ungar Publishing Co., 1952.

Putnam, James Jackson. *Addresses on Psycho-Analysis.* London: The International Psycho-Analytic P, 1921.

—. *Human Motives*. Boston: Little Brown and Co., 1915.

Winthrop, John. "City Upon a Hill." 1630. The Gilder Lehrman Institute of American History, 2013.

Anschluss and Immigration: Austria, America, and the Philippines in the Late 1930s

Dean J. Kotlowski

At a press conference on 15 March 1938, President Franklin D. Roosevelt found himself addressing two seemingly unrelated international issues. Three days earlier, Nazi Germany had absorbed Austria to form an *Anschluss* or union between the two German-speaking lands. Adolf Hitler's move into Austria was, according to Hugh R. Wilson, the United States ambassador in Berlin, "the greatest success" of his five-year-old regime (United States Department of State, *FRUS* 462). In Washington, reporters asked FDR if Austria had, in the view of the U.S. government, "ceased to exist as an independent nation" (Roosevelt, *PPC* 225). Roosevelt refused to comment (Roosevelt, *PPC* 226). Later in the press conference, the president received a question about Paul V. McNutt, former governor of Indiana and current United States high commissioner to the Philippines, who had recommended a revision of the timetable and terms for Philippine independence. Although McNutt favored keeping America's Asian colony, FDR declined to discuss the matter. By law, the president noted, the Philippines would become an independent nation in 1946 and "we may none of us be alive at that time" (Roosevelt, *PPC* 227). The remark was tragically ironic, for Roosevelt would die in 1945.

This press conference proved ironic in another way: During the late 1930s, United States-Austrian relations overlapped in the Philippines on two critical and somewhat related issues, that is, the *Anschluss* and the movement of Austrian Jews to Manila. The *Anschluss* resulted in the violent repression of Austrian Jews which, in turn, spurred Jews to leave Germany in ever greater numbers. The opening of the Philippines to refugees was largely due to McNutt who, from his position as high commissioner, helped 1,300 Austrian and German Jews secure visas to flee Nazi Germany and arrive in Manila. The fate of these refugees has received attention in *Escape to Manila: From Nazi Tyranny to Japanese Terror* (2003) by Frank Ephraim (himself one of the refugees), in an article in *Diplomatic History*, and in the documentary film *Rescue in the Philippines: Refuge from the Holocaust*, which aired on public television stations across the United States in 2013. Less known, at least to popular audiences, was McNutt's determination to deny official recognition to the *Anschluss* despite pressure from the German counsel in Manila.

Examining McNutt's tenure as high commissioner allows one to explore relations between the United States and Austria through the prism of empire, that is, the aggressive, racially-defined empire the Nazis were establishing in Europe and the twilight of American colonialism in the Philippines. Put another way, while Austria was losing its independence to Germany, the Philippines was on the road to receiving its independence from the United States. Both developments intersected following the *Anschluss*, as McNutt struggled to help Jewish refugees find safe haven in Manila.

ANSCHLUSS AND AFTERMATH

The *Anschluss* between Germany and Austria came as no surprise to foreign policy makers in Washington. As early as January 1938, reports from the U.S. embassy in Berlin warned that "some development" in "the Austrian question" was "relatively imminent" (*FRUS* 384). When Germany annexed Austria, many Americans expressed indignation. "Newspapers denounced the Nazi takeover," the historian Arnold A. Offner has written, "and even the isolationist Senator [William E.] Borah lamented Austria's loss of independence" (234). During a meeting with Undersecretary of State Sumner Welles, the State Department official most trusted by FDR, the German ambassador to the United States Hans Heinrich Dieckhoff vented about the negative press coverage. Insisting that Austria "has always desired an *Anschluss* with Germany," Dieckhoff complained "that no matter what Germany did, the rest of the world was always ready to inveigh against her" (*FRUS* 442-43). Critics of the *Anschluss* also picketed the German Consulate General in New York, much to the annoyance of the German embassy in Washington (*FRUS* 464).

Many Americans ignored the *Anschluss*. With memories of the First World War still fresh, the national mood in the United States had turned toward isolationism and pacifism. "As war clouds gathered in the early 1930s," the historian John E. Wiltz has observed, "Americans became obsessed with desire to avoid repetition of the quixotic crusade of 1917-18" (*In Search* 3-4). FDR had sensed such sentiments just months before Germany's absorption of Austria. In October 1937, the president spoke in Chicago, home of the "obstreperously isolationist *Chicago Tribune,*" where he likened recent acts of international aggression—Hitler's reoccupation of the Rhineland, Japan's invasion of China, and Italy's conquest of Ethiopia—to an epidemic that required a "quarantine" of the aggressor nations (Kennedy 404). While "public reaction to the address was generally favorable," isolationists attacked Roosevelt, who retreated by declining to specify what he meant by "quarantine" (Gellman 148). Two months later, the Japanese sinking of the American gunboat U.S.S. *Panay* in China's Yangtze River stirred few cries for war. To the contrary, Representative Maury Maverick, Democrat of Texas, averred: "We should learn that it is about time for us to mind our own business" (Kennedy 402). Roosevelt disagreed, albeit weakly. Early in 1938, he offered to host a conference at which several small nations would draft standards for international relations. Dismissing the proposal as "preposterous" and "likely to excite the derision of Germany and Italy" (Kennedy 407), British Prime Minister Neville Chamberlain proceeded with his own policy of appeasing Germany and Italy (Offner 229-33).

President Franklin D. Roosevelt in 1938. Library of Congress, Prints & Photographs Division, photograph by Harris & Ewing, [reproduction number: LC-DIG-hec-47384].

The U.S. government responded to the *Anschluss* in a predictably cautious way. Welles warned Dieckhoff that "new acts of repression and persecution" by the German government against Austrians would inflame American public opinion against Germany (*FRUS* 445). Yet the United States lacked allies, and the will, to force Hitler to withdraw his troops from Austria. British foreign secretary Lord Halifax accepted the absorption of Austria "into the German Reich" as a "foregone conclusion" (*FRUS* 449). Under these circumstances, the United States did little, save to register its disapproval of the *Anschluss* via words and diplomatic protocol. Secretary of State Cordell Hull called "the Austrian incident" a "matter of serious concern" to the United States, and Assistant Secretary of State George Messersmith proposed a response (*FRUS* 457). Observing that the United States had declined to recognize either the Japanese occupation of Manchuria or the Italian takeover over Ethiopia, Messersmith suggested that the United States could deny recognition to the Austro-German union by refusing to transform its embassy in Vienna into a regional consulate. The fact that the position of U.S. minister to Austria had been vacant made this course of action both expedient and appealing (*FRUS* 452). Non-recognition became the American policy—for four weeks. Following a plebiscite on 10 April 1938, in which 99.02 percent of Germans and 99.75 percent of Austrians voted in favor of the *Anschluss*, the U.S. government accepted reality, closed its legation in Vienna, and converted the embassy's consular division into a U.S. consulate. In so doing, it acknowledged that Vienna was no longer the capital of an independent nation but a provincial city within an enlarged Germany (*FRUS* 476-77).

The plebiscite requires further explanation, for this tactic would be copied months later in the Philippines. Contrary to the impression later generated by Hollywood in *The Sound of Music* (and by Winston Churchill, who wrote of the "Rape of Austria"), Austrians were not overwhelmingly opposed to fascism or Nazism (Churchill 232-50). The right-of-center, authoritarian ministries of Engelbert Dolfuss (1932-1934) and Kurt von Schuschnigg (1934-1938) struggled to defend Austrian independence by suppressing an indigenous Nazi movement that was growing in strength and favorable toward union with Germany. Sentiments for joining all German-speaking peoples within a greater Reich predated Hitler but he pushed the project strongly, in part because he was Austrian by birth. Weaknesses in the Austrian state and economy following the First World War, Hitler's own connections to Austria, and his success in nullifying restrictions in the postwar peace settlement all lifted the German dictator's standing among the non-Jewish population of Austria. Immediately following the *Anschluss*, Hitler visited Austria where multitudes cheered him. "In beautiful spring weather," the historian Ian Kershaw has written, "Hitler addressed a vast, delirious crowd, estimated at a quarter of a million people, in Vienna's Heldenplatz" (81). A month later, he won ratification of the *Anschluss* via plebiscite, a device he had used earlier to legitimize Nazi policies. "Whatever the undoubted manipulative methods, ballot-rigging, and pressure to conform which helped produce it," Kershaw observed, there was "genuine support for Hitler's action" (83). In Austria, "the verdict reflected Austrian opinion," although in a free election the margin probably "would not have been so high" (Jelavich 224).

The consequences of Germany's occupation of Austria soon became evident to Vienna's Jewish population. The Nazis inflicted some of the same terrors and indignities on Austrian Jews that they had on German Jews. They robbed Jews, some of whom "were dragged from offices, shops, or homes and forced to scrub the pavements in 'cleaning squads'" (Kershaw 84). According to journalist William L. Shirer, "they worked on their hands and knees with jeering storm troopers standing over them" (477). Under these circumstances, many Jews sought to flee the country. But, because of the *Anschluss*, Germany now had a larger Jewish population to resettle. "There were still possibly some 360,000 Jews left in Germany at the beginning of 1938," the historian Paul Bartrop has explained, "and the *Anschluss* added another 180,000, making a total of 540,000—a figure which was about 40,000 higher than in 1933" (Bartrop 130). To make matters worse, the most obvious destination for resettlement, the British mandate of Palestine, was not an option because the government in London, mindful of Arab sentiments, had limited the flow of Jewish immigration into Palestine (Kotlowski, "Finding Havens" 166).

FDR responded skittishly to these developments. He tightened the screws on Austria by ending its trade advantages with the United States and insisting that Germany assume responsibility for paying Austrian debts to American firms (Dallek 158; Offner 238-39). And twelve days after the *Anschluss*, Roosevelt called upon the nations of the world to form "a special committee for the purpose of facilitating the emigration from Austria and presumably from Germany of political refugees." He went so far as to urge "speedy cooperative effort" in order to halt "widespread human suffering" (Roosevelt, *PPA* 169). FDR's good friend—and love interest, some said—Dorothy Schiff praised the statement for bringing "courage again and hope" to "the Jews of Germany and Austria." Intelligent, Republican, Jewish, and wealthy (she later purchased the *New York Post*), Schiff swelled with pride, she confided to the president, "that it was our government—through you—that has pointed the way" (Schiff to FDR 30 March 1938).

Yet Roosevelt's leadership proved half-hearted at best and cynical at worst. By referring to "political refugees" rather than to Jews (or immigrants generally), FDR's statement bowed to popular prejudices, for many Americans resisted opening their country to foreign-born workers, especially Jews. Decades later, Schiff recalled a mischievous, if not malevolent, scheme broached by the president to thwart the entrance of Jewish refugees into the United States. FDR planned to ask Rabbi Stephen Wise, who had "begged" for the admission of European Jews, and White House speech-writer Samuel I. Rosenman, a Jew who opposed opening the United States to refugees, "to get together with a program to submit to him" knowing these two men would never be able to agree on a common course of action. After describing the ploy, Roosevelt, Schiff remembered, "threw his head back and laughed. Appalled, I said nothing" (Schiff, Memorandum 22 January 1979).

FDR was not as insensitive as his off-hand remark to Schiff suggested. He certainly was no anti-Semite. The president appointed a number of Jews to ranking positions in his administration and in so doing won the support of Jewish voters. Indeed, during the 1930s, some American Jews professed to believe in three things: (1) "*diese welt*" (or "this world"), (2) "*jener welt*" (or "the world to come") and (3) "Roosevelt" (Hershfield). Nevertheless, Roosevelt knew that labor unions, a core constituency group in his Democratic Party, "did not wish large numbers of poor refugees to come into the country" during a time of economic depression. FDR also understood that many Americans had been drawn to the ideas of the Detroit-area priest Father Charles Coughlin, whose radio speeches blended prescriptions for monetary reform with anti-Semitism (Schiff, Memorandum 22 January 1979). Other Americans were overtly and indiscriminately xenophobic. Maury Maverick remarked that during the American war for independence, "Lafayette came over here, and Baron von Steuben, also a foreigner, came to train our Revolutionary troops, and we were glad to have them." But, he emphasized, "we do not like foreigners any more" (Wiltz, *From Isolation* 6). Aware of such opinions, Roosevelt moved cautiously on the refugee issue.

Anti-immigrant and anti-Semitic sentiments at the grassroots level filtered upward to the highest echelons of the U.S. government, reinforcing a formidable set of obstacles for Jews seeking to enter the United States. They included a restrictive policy of annual quotas enshrined in the Immigration Act of 1924; anti-refugee sentiments in Congress, which would have to enact any changes to immigration law; bureaucratic inertia and anti-Semitism at the Department of State; and the Immigration Act of 1917, which forbade aliens from entering the United States if they were unable to support themselves and "likely to become a public charge" (Breitman and Kraut 7). When enforced strictly, that last stipulation demanded that immigrants prove not that they possessed the minimal "skills required for constructive employment," but that they were likely to obtain something far-from-certain during the 1930s: "a job under current market conditions" (Breitman and Kraut 7-8). The layers of official impediments formed an almost impregnable edifice that the historian David Wyman likened to paper walls (vii-xi).

Given such obstacles at home, FDR looked abroad for solutions to the Jewish refugee crisis. He found few. In calling for the establishment of a special international committee to assist refugees, Roosevelt stipulated that "no country would be expected or asked to receive a greater number of immigrants than is permitted by its existing legislation" (Roosevelt, *PPA* 169). The president's transparent attempt to uphold current U.S. law, with all its restrictions, encouraged other nations to do likewise. When representatives from Australia, New Zealand, the Americas and Europe met in Evian-les-Bains, France in July 1938 to address the refugee problem "delegate after delegate came to the podium to insist that their nation's record on immigration was unassailable and that the restrictions their governments had imposed were meant only to make sure refugees did not become public charges" (Wells 5). Concerns about unemployment, along with anti-Semitism, xenophobia and indifference, limited the assistance to which governments were willing to commit and hamstrung the efforts of the Intergovernmental Committee on Political Refugees, which had been formed following the Evian conference (Breitman and Kraut 56-77). The British ambassador to the United States admitted that his government was having "as much difficulty in convincing the British colonies and dominions" to act as the U.S. government would, if the Roosevelt administration asked the governors of Nevada and Montana to accept European refugees (*FRUS* 831).

U.S. officials gather at a White House meeting on refugees, 13 April 1938.
Left to right: Professor Joseph P. Chamberlain; Assistant Secretary of State George S. Messersmith; Rabbi Stephen S. Wise; Henry Morgenthau, Sr.; Reverend Samuel Cavert; Reverend Michael J. Ready; Secretary of Labor Frances Perkins; and Lewis Kenedy. *Library of Congress, Prints & Photographs Division, photograph by Harris & Ewing,* [reproduction number: LC-DIG-hec-24424].

Not unlike the United States, Australia and Canada maintained restrictive policies. Australia's response to the refugee crisis betrayed little consistency "other than that of restricting Jewish entry" (Bartrop, "Indifference" 149). The Canadian government expressed sympathy for Jews without accepting significant numbers of them. Upon learning of that a young Jewish woman faced deportation to Germany, Prime Minister William Lyon Mackenzie King wrote in his diary: "It was inhuman for our Department of Immigration to allow that child to be returned. I feel we must do something as a country to admit some of these refugees" (14 November 1938). Yet the government in Ottawa had raised concern about the "feasibility" of forming an international refugee committee outside of the League of Nations and it cited "difficult problems under Canadian immigration laws" with respect to accepting Austrian and German Jews (*FRUS* 753). During the Second World War, King privately spoke of the need to welcome Jewish refugees in order to populate his country's "large waste spaces" but he said little about the issue in public, lest it unsettle native-born Canadians "on the eve of an election" (Levine 364-65). As a result, Canada did little. According to historians Irving Abella and Harold Topper, "when confronted with the Jewish problem, the response of the government, the civil service and, indeed, much of the public wavered somewhere between indifference and hostility" (Foster 81).

In this setting, the U.S. and British governments explored the possibility of resettling Jewish refugees in their colonies and client states. At Evian, historian Henry Feingold has written, "the British had not displayed much enthusiasm for using British possessions in Africa" (104). Accordingly, Roosevelt considered other locales in Africa, including the Portuguese and French colonies of Angola and Madagascar, respectively (Breitman and Kraut 63). But Myron Taylor, the president's representative to the Intergovernmental Committee on Political Refugees, deemed resettlement proposals impracticable since "cooperation must be developed with countries of immigration, land must be purchased, [and] water supply, roads and housing must be provided." Such ventures required tremendous "capital investment" that few governments or private relief agencies would or could provide (Taylor 272). And talk of bringing refugees to South America—British Guiana—never progressed very far, partly because of FDR's concern that European Jews would be unable to adjust to the warm climate (Morgenthau 6).

Interestingly, a pair of small refugee havens emerged, both in tropical countries: the Dominican Republic and the Philippines. Seeking to refurbish his international reputation after sanctioning a massacre of Haitians, Dominican dictator Rafael Trujillo responded favorably to the needs of refugees. He transferred a tract of land at Sosúa, on his country's northern coast, to the Dominican Republic Settlement Association, which worked alongside the American Jewish Joint Distribution Committee to welcome the first wave of refugees in 1940. This "unconventional experiment saved lives" despite its "small size and the numerous obstacles arrayed against it" (Wells xix). Nearly 1,000 Austrian and German Jews went to Sosúa, which is about the same number who made it to Manila during the same period of time.

THE PHILIPPINES AS A REFUGEE HAVEN

The Philippines became a haven for Austrian and German Jews largely due to the efforts of Paul McNutt. A presence on the national political stage from the mid-1920s until his death in 1955, McNutt was acquainted with the exercise of power, which proved vital when he confronted the refugee crisis. McNutt had been both a state (1926-1927) and national (1928-1929) commander of the American Legion, the chief veterans' organization to emerge in the United States following the First World War. As governor of Indiana (1933-1937), he backed the New Deal and led his state forcefully before serving Presidents Franklin D. Roosevelt and Harry S. Truman as high commissioner to the Philippines (1937-1939 and 1945-1946), federal security administrator (1939-1945), chair of the War Manpower Commission (1942-1945) and ambassador to the Philippines (1946-1947). McNutt's hope to be the Democratic nominee for president in 1940 ended with FDR's nomination for a third term. He next sought the nomination for vice president, until Roosevelt indicated his preference for Secretary of Agriculture Henry A. Wallace. After the Second World War, McNutt returned to the Philippines where he prepared the archipelago for independence. His political legacy thus became entwined with the fate of both the Philippines and the refugees who immigrated there (Kotlowski, *Paul V. McNutt* 1-11).

Stemming from his unique background as a soldier in the First World War, leader in veterans' politics, state executive, and colonial administrator, McNutt developed strong internationalist sentiments and a harsh antipathy toward Nazi Germany and its allies. By serving as an officer during the First World War without seeing combat overseas, he witnessed the promise of patriotic sacrifice without experiencing firsthand the horrors of mechanized warfare. McNutt celebrated his military service and joined the American Legion. The ideology of the Legion encouraged him to fight Communism and other forms of radicalism and to advocate military preparedness and greater expenditure on arms in order to protect the American homeland. Throughout his career, McNutt held a realistic view of international relations. He dismissed disarmament treaties and efforts to promote peace by outlawing war as misguided for they underestimated the determination of nations to pursue their own self-interest. Faced with such realities, the United

States had to be militarily strong and actively engaged in international politics. As the high commissioner in Manila during the late 1930s, McNutt urged the U.S. government to retain the Philippines as an outpost of American power rather than grant the colony independence and leave it vulnerable to Japan (Kotlowski, "First Cold War Liberal" 544-51, 560-66).

As governor of Indiana, McNutt emerged as one of the earliest critics of Hitler's dictatorship. Hitler became chancellor of Germany on 30 January 1933, exactly three weeks after McNutt had taken office in Indianapolis. Throughout 1933, McNutt received almost daily reminders about the Nazi regime in the *Indianapolis Times*, the most progressive-minded newspaper in the state capital, which ran stories under such headlines as "Jews Beset by Hate and Ruin in Germany" (Kotlowski, *Paul V. McNutt* 237). McNutt also read memoranda from Jewish groups detailing Nazi atrocities. At the end of one report, he jotted: "Are we to join the traitors to the human brotherhood who prey upon the lives and souls of other men, or are we to enlist in the war for justice, a war which is never done!" (Kotlowski, *Paul V. McNutt* 237). Unusual for the time, McNutt, a Methodist, openly admired Jewish history and culture. "The faith of the Israelites has made them a people, whom forty centuries have not been able to destroy," he stressed (Kotlowski, *Paul V. McNutt* 237). And in March 1933, McNutt traveled to Chicago where he addressed "one of the first anti-Nazi meetings in the country" and characterized the Nazi assault on Jews as an "injustice" contrary to "morality and humanity." "For the second time in my life," this veteran of the First World War announced, "I rise to protest against the acts of the German government" (Kotlowski, *Paul V. McNutt* 237-38).

McNutt's philio-Semitism derived from several sources. First, as a boy, he had been bullied, and that may have sparked his sympathy for victims of persecution. Second, his family had ties to freemasonry, a movement that had experienced discrimination over the course of American and European history. Third, McNutt himself had connections to Jews, one of whom, Jacob Weiss, was a political partner in Indiana. Fourth, McNutt championed religious tolerance for idealistic as well as political reasons. Although the American Legion practiced racial segregation, the organization was open to all veterans of the Great War regardless of race, ancestry or religion, and McNutt worked to keep it that way. And while McNutt recognized that anti-Semitism motivated many voters, his Democratic Party had been more welcoming of immigrants than its Republican counterpart had been. Indeed, Jews comprised an important constituency in the reform coalitions assembled by him and FDR (Kotlowski, "Breaching" 867-77). It also should be noted that McNutt, unlike Roosevelt, was not closely associated with the rights of workers, for he had deployed National Guard troops to quell labor unrest during his years as governor. Accordingly, he would not have been unduly sensitive to Big Labor's objections to admitting greater numbers of immigrants (Kotlowski, *Paul V. McNutt* 189-91). Whatever its origin or origins, McNutt's criticism of Nazi persecution contrasted with the silence of FDR; in 1933, the president insisted that Germany's mistreatment of Jews was "not a governmental affair" and that he could "do nothing" to stop it (Offner 68). As Roosevelt explained, the best option available to the United States was using "personal and unofficial influence to moderate conditions" in Germany (Offner 68).

With respect to Jews, McNutt voiced an inclusive perspective, acknowledging Jewish contributions to building America and envisioning Jews as allies in the effort to establish an orderly and just world. While speaking in Chicago, he chastised the Nazi assault on Jews: "No government can long endure that fails to guarantee to its people the right to live as normal human beings. The present government of Germany thus writes its own destruction" (Kotlowski, *Paul V. McNutt* 239). McNutt was implicitly warning his fellow countrymen to refrain from Nazi-style persecutions, lest they too write their own epitaph. As the 1930s wore on, McNutt praised Jewish philanthropic institutions as one progenitor of New Deal social reforms (Kotlowski, *Paul V. McNutt* 239). He also saw Jews as a key protagonist in the international struggle against tyranny. "Wherever liberalism weakens and an opportunity is offered to a would-be dictator," he declared in 1939, "anti-Semitism is used to create a 'group will' to serve the dictator's ambition" (Kotlowski, *Paul V. McNutt* 239).

McNutt confronted the Nazis directly when he became high commissioner to the Philippines in 1937. In Manila, McNutt sought to protect American prestige in Asia, assert U.S. sovereignty over the Philippines and confront the ambitions of dictatorial regimes. He clashed with the German consul in Manila, Gustav Adolf Sakowski, who was striving to raise his nation's profile in the Philippines. Before McNutt's arrival in Manila, Sakowski founded the "German-Filipino Friendship Association" in order to broaden contacts between both peoples and to "introduce German culture" into the Philippines ("Germany" 5). In March 1938, the German consul sought to arrange a plebiscite among German and Austrian nationals in order to ratify the *Anschluss*. McNutt objected, whereupon Sakowski staged a shipboard meeting, beyond Philippine waters, at which three hundred Germans and Austrians pledged allegiance to their enlarged Fatherland (Kotlowski, *Paul V. McNutt* 240). McNutt replied "more sharply" when Sakowski urged the German Club of Manila to expel its Jewish members. He warned the consul not to "reorganize the German club along Nazi principles," and emphasized that "the American government guarantees religious tolerance and freedom from persecution to all persons living under its flag" ("Untitled Narrative"). Sakowski again backed down by allowing the club to determine its membership. In reacting to such incidents, which one State Department official labeled "indiscrete" and "embarrassing," McNutt simultaneously defended U.S. sovereignty and ideals, especially regarding the rights of religious minorities (Moffat, Diary 22 August 1938).

Secretary of State Cordell Hull (left) and United States High Commissioner to the Philippines Paul V. McNutt (right) meet in Washington, D.C., 23 February 1938. *Library of Congress, Prints & Photographs Division, photograph by Harris & Ewing* [reproduction number: LC-DIG-hec- 24103].

McNutt further demonstrated his concern by allowing Jewish refugees to settle in Manila. He was able to do so partly because the Philippines was in a state of transition. During the 1930s, the Philippines had progressed from being a U.S. colony to a semi-autonomous "commonwealth" slated to become fully independent in 1946. Beginning in 1935, Filipinos exercised control over their internal affairs and elected their own president while the United States retained sovereignty over the islands, represented in Manila by a high commissioner (Kotlowski, "Independence" 504-09). For the Philippines, then, the 1930s was an era of political change and readjustment. Immigration policy was a case in point. America's 1917 Immigration Act applied to entrants to the Philippines but its 1924 Act did not. Moreover, the Philippines had no immigration laws of its own, and enforcement of U.S. immigration law in the archipelago had been lax. This was one of the problems facing both McNutt and Manuel L. Quezon, who was elected president of the Philippines in 1935. Fortunately, these men forged a partnership which facilitated the refugee venture (Kotlowski, "Independence" 509-11).

The Philippines gradually emerged as a refugee haven. In 1937, twenty-eight German Jewish families fled Shanghai, China, and arrived in Manila. McNutt supported their entrance by waiving U.S. visa requirements, one of the few powers still held by the high commissioner. In 1938 he went further. During a brief visit to Washington, McNutt discussed a larger refugee venture with leaders of the American Jewish Joint Distribution Committee and the Refugee Economic Corporation (REC) which "specialized in creating Jewish settlements" in countries willing to accept refugees (Ephraim 27). McNutt endorsed the REC's project, provided that the Jewish community of Manila administered it. The constraints of the law, the danger of interference by the Department of State, and the volatility of public opinion on the subject of refugees all forced McNutt to insist that the émigrés be able to support themselves financially. The refugee committee in Manila, headed by the cigar manufacturer Philip Frieder, agreed. Frieder's committee compiled a list of categories of occupations and the number of Jews to be admitted in each grouping. Doctors, mechanics, accountants, barbers, engineers and a rabbi were among the jobs appearing on the committee's list. Manila's Jewish community thus assisted refugees in a way that promised to bolster its own economic vitality and social cohesion (Kotlowski, *Paul V. McNutt* 241-45).

The process for immigrating to, and settling in, the Philippines was straightforward. The chief Jewish relief agency in Germany accepted applications and forwarded them to the REC, which passed them on to the committee in Manila. Frieder and his team studied the applications and sent names to the Philippine government for approval. After applicants had demonstrated that they were unlikely to become a public charge, the State Department issued a visa from the appropriate consular office. McNutt stressed that the right sort of refugees be admitted to the Philippines, that is, people with skills who would arrive in manageable numbers. In so doing, he used laws designed to restrict immigration to bring Jewish professionals to Manila (Kotlowski, *Paul V. McNutt* 245-46). In the meantime, Philip Frieder and his brothers, especially Alex and Herbert, played an instrumental role in welcoming refugees to Manila. "We had open house for the refugees every Friday night," Alice Weston, Alex Frieder's daughter, recalled, "and the table was piled high with fried chicken and orchids from the garden" (*Rescue in the Philippines*). To avoid becoming public charges, some refugees took odd jobs or performed unfamiliar tasks. "My mother supplemented the income by taking in borders," Brigitta Welisch Wachs, an Austrian refugee, remembered, "and the interesting part about that was in Europe my mother never went into the kitchen or cooked or anything because they had a cook" (*Rescue in the Philippines*).

Austria occupied an important place in the refugee venture, even though McNutt's own ties to Austria proved minimal. He apparently visited the country once, during a trip to Europe with the American Legion in 1929 (Kotlowski, *Paul V. McNutt* 107). Nevertheless, many of the refugees who went to Manila came from Austria. During 1938 and 1939, word had spread in Vienna's Jewish community "about the possibility of entering the Philippines" as prelude to "immigrating to the United States" (Ephraim 27). Arrival in America, as Frank Ephraim explained, "was always the ultimate goal of Jewish refugees from Europe, and any possible avenue was eagerly explored" (27).

One Austrian Jew who made it to Manila, and then to America, was orchestra conductor Herbert Zipper. Born in Vienna in 1904 into a middle-class family, Zipper studied piano, "attended every concert and opera he could," and played music (Cummins 35). After completing a course of study at the State Academy of Music and the Performing Arts in 1929, he became a "musical gypsy" who took jobs "wherever he could find them" during the early years of the Depression (Cummins 54). He found work as a conductor in Germany, until Hitler's appointment as chancellor in 1933 forced him to return to Vienna, where he stayed until 1938. "The years from June of 1933 to March of 1938 were for Zipper years of feverish creativity and profound dismay," his biographer has written, as he composed music for the "underground theaters which sprang up in Vienna" in defiance of the Dolfuss and Schuschnigg regimes (Cummins 62, 66). Following the *Anschluss*, Zipper was arrested and sent to the concentration camp at Dachau, where he endured "brutality, hunger, terror, humiliation and misery" (Cummins 77). Undaunted, he comforted the other inmates by reciting poetry and forming a small orchestra with makeshift instruments (Cummins 83-86). At the end of 1938, the Nazis transferred Zipper to their camp at Buchenwald. But being held under the classification "protective custody" and "having a prosperous father" living abroad helped Zipper (Cummins 104). A prisoner in Zipper's category could be freed if he had a foreign country to immigrate to. Thanks to McNutt, Zipper did. And coming from a family with means, he was able to meet the financial requirements for entrance to the Philippines.

In many ways, Manila became an ideal location for Zipper. The conductor of the Manila Symphony had died, meaning that Zipper had a position waiting for him. He also reconnected with, and eventually married, his love interest, the dancer Trudl Dubsky, who "had gone to Manila in 1937 to serve as director of a dance studio" and to teach at the University of the Philippines (Cummins 115). Frank Ephraim described Zipper's welcome as almost royal: "Zipper was introduced to Manila's musical circles with a large reception at the stately home of the [politically influential family of] Benito Legarda" (56). Yet he had to adjust to a new land and life-style characterized by an "exotic countryside, a foreign culture, a totally different architecture and means of transportation, radically different trees and flowers, [and] visits from high government officials seeking his advice" (Cummins 120). As mentioned, the destination of choice for many Austrian and German Jews remained the United States, to where Zipper's parents and two of his siblings had immigrated in 1939 and 1940. Like many Jewish refugees to Manila, Zipper survived the Japanese occupation of the Philippines and then settled in America, where he conducted orchestras and promoted music education among young people (Cummins 120, 162; *Never Give Up*).

As Zipper and the other refugees came to Manila in 1938 and 1939, Manuel Quezon supported their entrance and eased their resettlement—to a point. The Philippine president was sympathetic to the plight of Austrian and German Jews, for he had no affinity with Nazi racial policies. Indeed, he had made a number of friends among American Jews who, like Filipinos, had experienced their share of prejudice. And in a goodwill gesture, Quezon gave the refugees part of his country estate for use as a farm (Ephraim 68). He also sought to bolster his nation economically by admitting skilled immigrants. Partly for that reason, he became attracted to a proposal to settle 10,000 Jewish refugees, over ten years, on the island of Mindanao (Kotlowski, *Paul V. McNutt* 244-45).

The so-called Mindanao Plan never came to fruition. It originated in August 1938 when McNutt received a query from President Roosevelt about the possibility of allowing another two hundred Jewish families into the Philippines (Feingold 98). The outline of the plan emerged in December 1938, following *Kristallnacht*, the infamous pogrom during which Nazi thugs attacked synagogues and Jewish-owned property across Germany. *Kristallnacht* aroused sympathy for Jews among Americans and Filipinos and encouraged officials at the State Department to search anew for havens. "President Quezon has indicated willingness to set aside virgin lands [in Mindanao] for colonization by Jewish refugees who wish to engage in agriculture," Sumner Welles wrote the U.S. embassy in London. "This Government has indicated approval of such a project" (*FRUS* 870).

McNutt probably suggested opening Mindanao to Jews because Quezon proved somewhat passive on the refugee issue. The Philippine president had reason for caution. Filipinos had been troubled by the economic success of immigrants from China and by the recent arrival of Japanese émigrés. In this setting, Quezon vacillated, especially after McNutt left the Philippines in 1939 to become head of the Federal Security Agency and launch his presidential campaign. Large-scale resettlement on Mindanao also entailed numerous problems, such as the need to select land, train settlers, and locate transport ships. Influenced in part by such concerns, Quezon in 1940 signed an immigration bill mandating that no more than five hundred people from each nation be admitted to the Philippines per year. While the law allowed Quezon to admit non-quota immigrants, the Mindanao Plan faced an uncertain fate. The outbreak of war in Europe killed it completely (Kotlowski, *Paul V. McNutt* 247-51).

Although there is no evidence that McNutt could have salvaged the Mindanao Plan, his departure hurt the refugee project. After McNutt left Manila, Quezon to some extent succumbed to the opponents of increased immigration. Yet if Mindanao proved an illusionary haven, Manila between 1938 and 1939 became a real one for 1,300 Jews. Frank Ephraim stressed the significance of what had unfolded: "Between the leadership of the Frieder brothers and McNutt, Jewish lives were being saved" (58).

RETROSPECT

The story of Austria, America, and the Philippines in the late 1930s illustrates how events in Europe spanned three continents, making the global crisis of the late 1930s global in ways often overlooked. The *Anschluss* reconfigured power arrangements in central Europe to Hitler's advantage. This shift occurred with scant protest from a British government inclined toward appeasement and a generally passive U.S. administration. The international community fared little better in accepting Jews during the refugee crisis that followed. The borders of the western countries remained largely closed, though some of their colonies and client states proved another matter. While Roosevelt and Welles from Washington envisioned locales in Africa and Latin America as possible havens for European refugees, McNutt, Quezon, and the Frieder brothers successfully brought 1,300 Jews to the Philippines.

Although McNutt seldom discussed the refugee venture, it left a mark on him. Revelations about the extent of the Holocaust in 1945 simultaneously vindicated his earlier warnings about Nazism, hardened his stand against the Axis powers, and touched him in a visceral way. Addressing a Jewish audience in Miami, McNutt denounced "the German apparatus of terror, the concentration camps, [and] the murder-factories." His fury matched his demand that all "points of prejudice and hate" be extinguished. Yet McNutt's hatred for Nazism and Japanese militarism (also denounced in this speech) got out of hand. McNutt's prepared remarks in Miami, in which he assailed "the decimation of Europe's Jews," had been preceded by his extemporaneous advocacy, in Chattanooga, Tennessee, of the complete annihilation of the Japanese people. Even the title of the Miami address, in which he shared ideas for shaping the postwar world, echoed a familiar Nazi refrain: "Towards a Thousand Year Democracy" (Kotlowski, *Paul V. McNutt* 372).

Irony, a favorite theme of historians, pervades the story of McNutt and the refugees from Austria and Germany. Circumstances, such as the outbreak of the Second World War in 1939 and FDR's decision to seek a third term, cheated McNutt of the chief object of his ambition: the White House. The annals of American political history are filled with lists of long-forgotten, would-be presidents. Far rarer are the names of Americans who acted to save lives during the Holocaust. McNutt managed to fall within both categories. So, in recent years, this once-prominent FDR-era politico has begun to be remembered, not as a possible president or vice president, but as an actual rescuer of European Jews. It follows, too, that McNutt should be seen as a bridge between Austria, America and the Philippines during the late 1930s.

WORKS CITED

Bartrop, Paul R. "Indifference and Inconvenience: Jewish Refugees and Australia, 1933-45." *False Havens. The British Empire and the Holocaust*. Ed. Paul R. Bartrop. Lanham, MD: UP of America, 1995. 127-57.

Breitman, Richard and Alan M. Kraut. *American Refugee Policy and European Jewry, 1933-1945*. Bloomington: Indiana UP, 1987.

Churchill, Winston S. *The Second World War*. Vol. I. *The Gathering Storm*. Boston: Houghton Mifflin, 1948.

Cummins, Paul F. *Dachau Song*. New York: Peter Lang, 1992.

Dallek, Robert. *Franklin D. Roosevelt and American Foreign Policy, 1932-1945*. New York: Oxford UP, 1979.

Ephraim, Frank. *Escape to Manila. From Nazi Tyranny to Japanese Terror*. Urbana, IL: U of Illinois P, 2003.

Feingold, Henry. *The Politics of Rescue. The Roosevelt Administration and the Holocaust, 1933-1945*. New Brunswick, NJ: Rutgers UP, 1970.

Foster, Lois. "No Northern Option: Canada and Refugees from Nazism before the Second World War." *False Havens. The British Empire and the Holocaust*. Ed. in Paul R. Bartrop. Lanham, MD: UP of America, 1995. 79-98.

Gellman, Irwin F. *Secret Affairs: FDR, Cordell Hull, and Sumner Welles*. New York: Enigma, 1995.

"Germany and P. I.: Reich Consul in Manila Discusses Philippine-German Relations," *Philippine Herald Mid-Week Magazine*. 2 Sept. 1936: 5.

Hershfield, Nathan. Conversation with the Author. Cincinnati, OH. 13 Feb. 2005.

Jelavich, Barbara. *Modern Austria: Empire and Republic, 1815-1986*. New York: Cambridge UP, 1987.

Kennedy, David M. *Freedom From Fear: The American People in Depression and War, 1929-1945*. New York: Oxford UP, 1999.

Kershaw, Ian. *Hitler, 1936-1945: Nemesis*. New York: Norton, 2000.

King, William Lyon Mackenzie. Diaries. Ottawa: Library and Archives Canada, 14 Nov. 1938.

Kotlowski, Dean J. "Breaching the Paper Walls: Paul V. McNutt and Jewish Refugees to the Philippines, 1938-1939." *Diplomatic History* 33.5 (2009): 865-96.

—. "Finding Havens to Save Lives: Four Case Studies from the Jewish Refugee Crisis of the 1930s." *Genocide, Risk and Resilience: An Interdisciplinary Approach*. Eds. Bert Ingelaere, Stephan Parmentier, Jacques Haers and Barbara Segaert. New York: Palgrave Macmillan, 2013. 164-77.

—. "The First Cold War Liberal? Paul V. McNutt and the Idea of Security from the 1920s to the 1940s." *Journal of Policy History*. 23:4 (2011): 540-85.

—. "Independence or Not? Paul V. McNutt, Manuel L. Quezon, and the Reexamination of Philippine Independence, 1937-39." *International History Review* 32.3 (2010): 501-31.

—. *Paul V. McNutt and the Age of FDR*. Bloomington: Indiana UP, 2015.

Levine, Allan. *King: William Lyon Mackenzie King, A Life Guided by Destiny*. Toronto: Douglas & McIntyre, 2011.

Moffat, Jay Pierrepont. Diary. Box 211. Sumner Welles Papers. Hyde Park, New York: Franklin D. Roosevelt Library, 22 Aug. 1938.

Morgenthau, Henry. Unpublished Manuscript: "Refugees (Up to the Outbreak of War: 1938-39)." Folder: Book—Refugees. Box 406. Henry Morgenthau, Jr. Papers. Hyde Park, New York: Franklin D. Roosevelt Library, 1946.

Never Give Up: The Twentieth-Century Odyssey of Herbert Zipper. Santa Monica, CA: American Film Foundation, 1995 (DVD).

Offner, Arnold A. *American Appeasement: United States Foreign Policy and Germany, 1933-1938*. Cambridge, MA: Belknap P of Harvard UP, 1969.

Rescue in the Philippines: Refuge from the Holocaust. Frederick, MD: Three Roads Communications, 2013 (DVD).

Roosevelt, Franklin D. *Complete Presidential Press Conferences of Franklin D. Roosevelt*. Vols. XI-XII. New York: Da Capo, 1972. (Cited throughout as "*PPC*").

—. *The Public Papers and Addresses of Franklin D. Roosevelt: 1938*. New York: Macmillan, 1941. (Cited throughout as "*PPA*").

Schiff, Dorothy. Letter to FDR. Folder: Franklin D. Roosevelt 1937 to 18 Nov. 1980. Box 64. Dorothy Schiff Papers. New York: New York Public Library, 30 March 1938.

—. Memorandum. Folder: Israel (General) 1963-1987. Box 26. Dorothy Schiff Papers. New York Public Library, New York, New York, 22 Jan. 1979.

Shirer, William L. *The Rise and Fall of the Third Reich: A History of Nazi Germany*. New York: Fawcett, 1962.

Taylor, Myron (3 Oct. 1938). "Address before the Council on Foreign Relations in New York City." *Documentary History of the Franklin D. Roosevelt Presidency*. Vol. XII. *FDR's Protest of the Treatment of Jews in Germany*. Ed. George McJimsey. Lanham, MD: University Publications of America, 2003. 257-75.

United States Department of State. *Foreign Relations of the United States: Diplomatic Papers 1938*. Vol. I. Washington, DC: United States Government Printing Office, 1955. (Cited throughout as "*FRUS*").

"Untitled Narrative of McNutt's Tenure as High Commissioner. Folder: Articles for Administrator (Personal). Box 1. Information Files. Records of the Administrator of the Federal Security Agency, RG 235. College Park, MD: National Archives, Undated.

Wells, Allen. *Tropical Zion. General Trujillo, FDR, and the Jews of Sosúa*. Durham, NC: Duke UP, 2009.

Wiltz, John E. *From Isolation to War, 1931-1941*. Arlington Heights, IL: Harlan Davidson, 1968.

—. *In Search of Peace: The Senate Munitions Inquiry, 1934-36*. Baton Rouge: Louisiana State UP, 1963.

Wyman, David. *Paper Walls. America and the Refugee Crisis, 1938-1941*. New York: Pantheon, 1985.

AN AMERICAN IN ALLIED-OCCUPIED AUSTRIA: JOHN DOS PASSOS REPORTS ON "THE VIENNA FRONTIER"

BERNHARD WENZL

John Dos Passos reported on war-torn Austria in November 1945. Six months after its liberation from Nazi Germany, Austria had become a country occupied by more than 150,000 American, British, French and Russian soldiers. The four Allied Powers had set up their occupation zones, each of which was governed by a military commissioner.[1] They had also divided Vienna into four sectors, with the inner city being jointly administered by the Allied Control Council. So when the famous American novelist visited Austria, he encountered a country in ruins, whose population was suffering from cold, hunger and violence. More significantly, he experienced a country under occupation, meeting many American and Russian troops and witnessing the rising tension between the United States and the Soviet Union.

Dos Passos was on an assignment for *LIFE* magazine when he went to see Allied-occupied Austria in late 1945.[2] Prior to that, he had been working as a war correspondent for the popular weekly news magazine, covering American operations in the Pacific between December 1944 and April 1945.[3] After *LIFE* commissioned him to report the Nazi war criminal trials in Nuremberg, he sailed for Europe on 10 October. As the international military tribunal was scheduled to start on 20 November, there was enough time for him to tour France, Germany and Austria. On 8 November, he rode a jeep from a military camp in Bad Wiessee, Bavaria, through American-controlled territory to Linz, where he stayed for the night.[4] Next morning, he crossed the

---

[1] Eisterer has noted that "the military commissioners for Austria were named at the beginning of July: Marshall Ivan S. Konev for the Soviet occupation zone, Lieutenant General Richard L. McCreery for the British zone, General Mark W. Clark for the American zone, and General Marie-Emile Béthouart for the French zone" (197).

[2] Started by Henry Luce in 1936, *LIFE* was an American news magazine with a strong emphasis on photojournalism. It was published on a weekly basis until 1972, selling up to 13.5 million copies a week.

[3] See Townsend Ludington's authoritative biography for information on John Dos Passos's life during and after the Second World War.

[4] Hotel Wolfinger, situated at Hauptplatz 19, was then used by the U.S. Army as a hotel and mess for transient officers.

Enns Bridge into the Soviet zone and continued to Vienna. The few days that Dos Passos spent in Allied-occupied Austria formed the basis for the personal encounters and cultural experiences reported in "The Vienna Frontier," his informative article of 10 November.[5]

"The Vienna Frontier" was published in Dos Passos's *Tour of Duty*. Released by Houghton Mifflin on 20 August 1946, this book of reportage focuses on the war in the Pacific and the situation in postwar Europe. Its three parts comprise a total of fourteen first-person articles, six of them being revised reports previously printed by *LIFE*. A shortened version of Dos Passos's article about Allied-occupied Austria had appeared under the title "Vienna: Broken City" in the 4 March 1946 issue of the weekly news magazine.[6] The text of the report was illustrated with eleven black and white photographs of war-ravaged Vienna, ten of them credited to John Phillips[7] and one to the Associated Press. The first edition of *Tour of Duty* was issued with three decorations by Howard Baer in eight thousand copies and, after receiving many favorable reviews from the American press, sold exceptionally well.[8]

"The Vienna Frontier" opens with scenes evocative of the American myth of the frontier.[9] En route to Linz, Dos Passos passes a group of wretched Hungarians who return home in covered wagons. Similar to worn-out pioneers crossing the plains region in their prairie schooners, "they sat with their feet on the tongues of the broken-down farm wagons rigged with makeshift canvas covers, and jogged along in the rain. Beside them, in a confusion of bedding und cook stoves and pots and pans and cradles, hunched their women with their heads tied up in handkerchiefs and their ragged hollow-eyed children" (275). But unlike the hopeful settlers heading West in search of fertile lands, the pitiable Hungarians go east into a dark wasteland, an ever bleaker country full of rain, mist, and chill.

---

[5] For a detailed chronology of the trip to Austria see John Dos Passos's letters and diaries, edited by Townsend Ludington.

[6] Besides "Vienna: Broken City," *LIFE* published "The Atolls," "The American Marianas" and "Report from Nürnburg" (sic!) in 1945, and "Americans are Losing the Victory in Europe" and "Report on the Occupation" in 1946.

[7] John Phillips (1914-1996) was an Algerian-born photographer working for *LIFE* magazine from the 1930s to the 1950s. He is best known for his war photographs.

[8] Howard Baer (1929-1986) was an American cartoonist and illustrator working for *The New Yorker*, *Esquire* and *Colliers* before turning to painting in the late 1940s.

[9] Slotkin has claimed that "the Myth of the Frontier is our oldest and most characteristic myth, expressed in a body of literature, folklore, ritual, historiography, and polemics produced over a period of three centuries" (11).

Upon his arrival in freezing cold Linz, Dos Passos is even more overwhelmed by "the feeling of the frontier" (275). With the Danube River serving as a demarcation line between the Soviet and American occupation zones, the Upper Austrian capital is a divided city at the time. No wonder that Linz appears to him as a settlement in a borderland, as it were, the last outpost of civilization. While a few American soldiers are shown roaming the streets this side of the Nibelungen Bridge[10] in cowboy fashion, a U.S. military policeman is quoted dismissing the Russian troops on the other side as socially less advanced, culturally inferior people on a par with native Americans: "They are kinder crude [...] They don't seem eddicated [sic!]" (276). As a consequence, Dos Passos feels as if he is about to enter a wilderness inhabited by a more primitive tribe, when he leaves the American zone and crosses the Enns Bridge into the Soviet zone the next day.

Surprisingly enough, the Russian soldiers that Dos Passos watches on his way to Vienna are not presented as savages but characters from nineteenth-century novels. A Red Army officer with a red band on his cap resembles a boyar, a Russian landed nobleman, "bowling along in an ancient Victoria with a yellow wicker body" (277), while the man bundled up on the driver's seat appears as his serf, "the flat-faced izvozchik of all the droshkies in Russian literature" (277).[11] The sentimental stereotype of the crude yet soulful Slav persists as long as Dos Passos has no direct contact with the Soviet troops.[12] The rank-and-file soldiers standing along the road and "staring at you the while with a cow-like stare off the great steppes" (282) are described as "big-eyed young Slavs who had an appealing coltish look of being right out of the isba" (278). When he passes some Lower Austrian village crowded with Red Army soldiers, his own mental images get the better of him:

> The fir boughs and the flat Slav faces and the red and green decorations against the broken-down houses banked with snowdrifts yellow and pitted from the rain, and the way the Russians in their boots stood in a group under the arch as if they were about to break into song,

[10] The Nibelungen Bridge in Linz and the Enns Bridge in Enns were two of the few points connecting the Soviet and American occupation zones in Upper Austria.

[11] Izvozchik and isba are Russian terms meaning coachman and log house, respectively. They likely found their way into the report because Dos Passos had been reading Leo Tolstoy's *War and Peace* shortly before his trip (Carr 431).

[12] Beller and Leerssen have shown that Russian stereotypes in literature include uncouth boyars and serfs, refined imperial aristocrats, the Russian Soul and the Cold War agent (226-30).

> made me think of all the choruses in all Russian operas I've seen. It was amazing to find yourself so deep in Russia so soon. (279)

Once Dos Passos enters war-shattered Vienna, his view of the Soviet troops changes considerably. At first, it is hard for him to meet Red Army soldiers because communism is supposed to have had a devastating effect on society: "For nearly thirty years now the only view of the world outside the Soviet Union its citizens have had has been through the distorting prism of Marxist propaganda. Every Soviet citizen feels that a bitter two-way hostility exits between him and the capitalist world" (282). Dos Passos supposes that the Russian occupation troops keep their distance for fear that "any contact with foreigners will be misinterpreted by the dangerous snoopers of the NKVD" (282).[13] At last, a Russian-speaking officer of the United States Armed Forces introduces him to a Red Army major, "a typical broad-faced Ukrainian, short and deep-chested with light crinkly hair" (283) who teaches literature in school and is well-versed in twentieth-century American fiction. After taking supper in a hotel's private dining room, they become entangled in a political discussion about equality and democracy, which shows them at odds in terms of ideology. While the Soviet soldier is in favor of paying salaries according to a worker's value to society, arguing that "trying to even up the wages of a ditch digger with two left hands and an irreplaceable brain-worker was capitalist equalitarianism and a great mistake" (283), the Americans are stunned to hear how electoral campaigns are run in a one-party system: "In Russian elections they did not vote on policies, only on personalities. Of course, there was only one candidate, but there was discussion before the nominations. The campaign was not about a man's opinions, but about his qualifications. The voter wanted to know which was the most intelligent, most experienced, best educated man for the job" (284). When it comes to explaining his practice of ticket splitting in elections, Dos Passos is confronted with mistrust and incomprehension on the part of the Red Army major, finding him "as suspicious of his capitalist friends as a Connecticut farmer out with a bunch of bookmakers" (284).

A visit to the Vienna headquarters of the United States Armed Forces in Austria[14] confirms the twentieth-century stereotype of the Russians as sly

[13] The NKVD was a law enforcement agency in the Soviet Union, closely associated with the secret police and known for its political repression during Stalinism.

[14] The building of the Oesterreichische Nationalbank on Otto-Wagner-Platz served as the headquarters of the United States Armed Forces in Austria from 1945 to 1951.

communists.[15] The majority of the American soldiers that Dos Passos interviews is "thoroughly discouraged by their experiences with what they called the arrogance and the double dealing and the lack of regard for the rights of man of the Russians with whom they negotiated" (285). They share the view that the Western Allies have been tricked into accepting a situation in postwar Europe that puts them at a disadvantage: "The British and Americans began their game in the privacy of the Big Three conclaves at Tehran and Yalta and Potsdam by dealing out all the trumps to the Russians" (286).[16] A high-ranking officer sums up the way most Americans have come to feel towards the Soviets: "Every little item that comes up is considered by the Russians as part of their hand in the great international poker game. … We're not really qualified to play that game because we don't know the rules. What we've been trying to do is to get them to put their cards on the table and to tell us what they want, but that seems to be against their religion" (286). The most American of all card games is used throughout the entire passage to convey the risky nature of the postwar order and the inscrutable character of the Soviets.[17]

Although Vienna has seen much destruction in the war, Dos Passos presents the city as a home to entertainment and easy living. He reports that "in the royal palace the famous boys' choir that sang Mass so many Sunday mornings for the Habsburgs and the dignitaries of their court still sings the cheerful Schubert Masses" (281). He also observes that the theaters have reopened, concerts are played, and clubs put on songs and sketches. No matter how much the local population has suffered from the deprivations of war, it is noted that "the life that is starting up again in the ruins takes on a semblance of the old patterns" (280). Accordingly, the unheated coffeehouses are full of people in tattered clothes who engage in lively talk or read the newspapers over cups of ersatz coffee.

---

[15] See Powers for the history of American anticommunism and the stereotyping of Russians as sly communists.

[16] The Big Three, i.e. Joseph Stalin, Winston Churchill/Clement Attlee and Franklin D. Roosevelt/Harry S. Truman, convened in Tehran in November/December 1943, in Yalta in February 1945 and in Potsdam in July 1945 to discuss Europe's post-war reorganization.

[17] Piette has claimed that "it is in Vienna, carved up like Berlin into rival Allied zones, that Dos Passos glimpses the new Cold War city-frontier that would define the postwar. As a good prodigal politico, he gives credence to the rumours in Vienna that excoriate Soviet deviousness and superpower machinations in the 'great poker game' of the brand-new Cold War" (49).

In compliance with the nineteenth-century image of Vienna as a place of music and theater, the city is pervaded by a sense of staginess.[18] In front of the Allied Kommandatura, Dos Passos encounters civilians watching the changing of the guard, "waiting for the pageantry to clear away [and] looking at the military show with a certain rapture" (289).[19] A commotion that he witnesses at a police station in the French occupation zone has an unmistakable touch of theatricality. When a stocky young Russian without papers is arrested for pillaging, "there milled a crowd of Viennese bystanders and local plainclothes men with faces out of an old-fashioned Punch and Judy show" (291). Upon his return from a coffeehouse an hour later, Dos Passos finds "the same characters still grouped on either side of the counter. [...] The center of the stage was held by two Russian Military Police officers who were listening gravely with white impassive faces to a long explanation in German by one of the plainclothes men" (294). While the Austrian inspector is likened to "an elocution teacher trying to rehearse a high-school play when the cast is getting out of hand" (294), Dos Passos notes that "my interpreter whispered in my ear in the tone of a man translating the action of a play"(295).

The role that Austria will play in the future is illustrated by the scene in the police station. With the inspector communicating with Russian military policemen and French occupation troops, he fulfills the function of mediator between East and West. Austria's future position in foreign affairs is anticipated by a man whose speech Dos Passos happens to hear in a lecture hall: "Vienna as the capital of a new Austrian republic will find new life as an interpreter and filter between the eastern Europe that will grow up with its face turned toward Moscow and the western Europe that will group up with its face turned toward Washington" (281). The principal of a Vienna school states in the presence of Dos Passos that the students are taught foreign languages with the aim to better prepare them for what lies ahead of them: "We are intensifying the study of English and in the higher grades Russian" (290).

Dos Passos also reports on how Austrians view themselves and the Allied forces. Asked how he has managed to survive the political changes starting with the Anschluss, the school principal denies any support of the Nazi re-

---

[18] Zacharasiewicz has stated that Vienna is mostly presented by Americans as a place of music and dancing in the nineteenth century and as a place of medicine and psychoanalysis in the twentieth century (188).

[19] The Allied Kommandatura was located between 1945 and 1953 in the Palace of Justice on Schmerlingplatz and later moved to the Allied Control Council on Schwarzenbergplatz.

gime: "'Politics is alien to pedagogy', he answered stiffly, and made a little washing motion with his hands" (289). Intended to downplay the massive influence of Nazism on schools, his evasive reply and gesture are typical of many Austrians who act the innocent, suppress their guilt and even pretend to the status of victims as suggested by the Moscow Declaration.[20] A journalist informs Dos Passos about the reasons why the Austrians feel disappointed in the Allied Powers:

> They had expected too much of their liberators. They had expected the Americans to bring food and businesslike vigor in the management of affairs. They had expected the Russians to bring new ideas, new things, perhaps terrible things but new things. But neither had brought anything new or vigorous. There was nothing new in starvation and looting and murder and rape. There was nothing new in bureaucratic stagnation. (292)

Although the Austrians have changed their view of the Allied forces from liberators to occupiers, they are said to make a crucial distinction between Americans and Soviets. Whereas General Mark W. Clark and his soldiers are considered friends because they make an effort to build up Austria, Marshall Ivan S. Konev, "Herr Djeltov, the big bullnecked man from the Kremlin," (293) and Red Army troops are regarded as enemies since they decline to go through with the reconstruction plan.[21]

John Dos Passos's report on "The Vienna Frontier" is an article full of literary metaphors, cultural stereotypes and mental images well-known to contemporary American readers. It introduces war-ravaged Austria as a frontier country, portrays Red Army soldiers as crude Slavs and sly communists, and describes the bombed-out city of Vienna as a home to music and theater. Additionally, it suggests Austria's future role in international politics and documents the way most Austrians saw themselves and their liberators after the Second World War, ranging from their self-definition as Nazi victims to their characterization of Americans as friendly helpers and their identification of Russians as hostile obstructionists. Marked by its historical and

[20] Signed by the Foreign Secretaries of the United States, the United Kingdom and the Soviet Union on October 30, 1943, the Moscow Declaration calls Austria "the first free country to fall victim to Hitlerite aggression."

[21] Aleksei Sergeevich Zheltov (1904-1991) was a military commander and colonel general who served as the Soviet Union's deputy supreme commissioner in Austria between 1945 and 1950.

ideological context, the text of "The Vienna Frontier" not only reflects an American author's encounters and experiences with Allied-occupied Austria but also anticipates the atmosphere of the Cold War era in postwar Vienna.[22]

WORKS CITED

Carr, Virginia Spencer. *Dos Passos: A Life*. Northwestern UP, 2005.

Carafano, James Jay. *Waltzing into the Cold War: The Struggle for Occupied Austria*. Texas A & M UP, 2002.

Dos Passos, John. *Tour of Duty*. Houghton Mifflin Company, Boston, 1946.

—. "Vienna: Broken City." *LIFE* Magazine 20.9, 4 March 1946, 92-104.

Eisterer, Klaus. "Austria Under Allied Occupation." Ed. Rolf Steininger et al. *Austria in the Twentieth Century*. New Brunswick, NJ, 2002, 190-211.

Imagology. The Cultural Construction and Literary Representation of National Characters. Eds. Manfred Beller and Joep Leerssen. Amsterdam, 2007.

Ludington, Townsend. *John Dos Passos: A Twentieth-Century Odyssey*. New York, 1980.

—. *The Fourteenth Chronicle: Letters and Diaries of John Dos Passos*. Harvard Common P, 1973.

Piette, Adam. *The Literary Cold War, 1945 to Vietnam*. Edinburgh : Edinburgh UP, 2009.

Powers, Richard Gid. *Not Without Honor : The History of American Anticommunism*. Yale UP, 1998.

Slotkin, Richard. *Gunfighter Nation: The Myth of the Frontier in Twentieth-Century America*. New York 1992.

Zacharasiewicz, Waldemar. "Waltzing in the German Paris: American Encounters with Musical Vienna". Eds. Udo J. Hebel and Karl Ortseifen. *Transatlantic Encounters: Studies in European-American Relations. Presented to Winfried Herget*. Trier, 1995, 176-92.

[22] Carafano provides an overview of the early Cold War activities in Allied-occupied Austria.

In Sickness and in Health: *The Third Man*'s U.S.-Centered 'On Location' Movie Publicity and Austrian-U.S. Postwar Relations

Anne-Marie Scholz

Based upon a short novel by Graham Greene, the 1949 British-U.S. co-production *The Third Man*, set in postwar four power-occupied Vienna, tells the story of the naive American writer, Holly Martins (Joseph Cotten), who discovers the corrupt activities of his allegedly murdered American friend Harry Lime (Orson Welles), and reluctantly helps the British police officers, Calloway and Paine (Trevor Howard, Bernard Lee), apprehend Lime. Long considered a classic of postwar British cinema, the energetic transnational cultural politics that shaped the film's production and reception during the early years of the Cold War shed light on a heretofore underemphasized dimension of those politics: the struggle to define and control the role of American economic and entertainment culture in postwar Europe. While the British producers of the film, director Carol Reed and screenwriter Greene, countered accusations of anti-communism—presenting the Russian occupation of Vienna in a negative light, for example—with claims that entertaining audiences was their only goal (as Greene would write: "We had no desire to move people's political emotions. We wanted to entertain them, to frighten them a little, to make them laugh" [Greene 11]), a closer look at the film's production history reveals an important subtext that defines the influence of American economic and popular culture in terms of infection, corruption and disease rather than, as the U.S. co-producer of the film David O. Selznick would have preferred, as arbiter of democracy, health, economic opportunity and popular culture. Cold War politics were less interesting to the British filmmakers than the cultural politics of America's influence on and in Europe. How was the metaphor of infection linked to the influence of U.S. culture on postwar Europe and what solutions does the film pose to this peculiar dilemma? How did aspects of the film's publicity campaign wind up differing dramatically from the premises vis-à-vis the Cold War of the film itself? And how did German-speaking audiences respond to the conceptions of the U.S./Austrian relationship implied by the film and its publicity?

* * *

To conceptualize the influence of a particular culture on another in terms of disease and infection implies two things: completely asymmetrical power relationships on the one hand; on the other hand, an antidote, a way to limit the spread of the infection. In its plot, *The Third Man* works with this dynamic very effectively, positing a type of quarantining of Europe as a preliminary antidote to the new cultural influence of the United States. Space has to be placed between the disease and the subject. The influence of American culture is asymmetric and contagious in its nature. European culture must keep a distance, figure out its own role in the new power constellations of the Cold War world.

How is this link between contamination and American culture created in the film? The two U.S. leads play the major role here. Harry Lime, the quintessential American capitalist, comes to Vienna to enrich himself at the expense of the lives of vulnerable European children. He spreads disease and death rather than curing it by engaging in the sale of diluted penicillin, a lucrative business that frees him from the shackles of income tax and the IRS, that is, from responsibility for the well-being of the larger community. Yet his direct influence as a criminal is only a part of his function as 'disease' carrier. He also 'infects' his friends, Holly Martins and Anna Schmidt, whose search for the absent Harry reveals the extent to which they have been infected by his charm and amorality. Harry's absence in the film only makes his influence the greater; like disease, he spreads his negative influence invisibly and irrevocably. Harry Lime himself is also ill with ulcers and is running out of medicine. He is himself infected, and his infectedness is reflected in his moral philosophy: that "bloodshed" and "terror" are sources of power, influence and culture:

> You know what the fellow said—in Italy, for thirty years under the Borgias, they had warfare, terror, murder and bloodshed, but they produced Michelangelo, Leonardo da Vinci and the Renaissance. In Switzerland, they had brotherly love...five hundred years of democracy and peace—and what did that produce? The cuckoo clock. (*The Third Man*)

Health and cleanliness are linked to boredom and the puritanical bourgeois stasis of the cuckoo clock and Swiss culture. (Later, Welles would report that he had been told in no uncertain terms that the cuckoo clock was a German not a Swiss invention).

Harry Lime's hiding place in the film, the Vienna sewer system, suggests the subterranean and contaminating influence of his presence in the city. During the production of the film, Orson Welles, at heart a puritanical American, was afraid of being contaminated himself, and refused to enter the sewer system for any length of time. Director Carol Reed was forced to reconstruct the sewer in a London studio to accommodate Welles' inclination toward hypochondria (*Shadowing the Third Man*). The British Major Calloway, who doggedly pursues Lime, is able to enlist the help of Lime's friend Holly Martins only after showing him the diseased results of Lime's business in the local military hospital: the dying children. Once Holly Martins is enlisted in the task of apprehending Lime, Lime's diseased presence in Vienna can be eliminated. Martins shoots his friend in the Vienna sewer.

Holly Martins, the American 'anti-hero' in the film, in his search for his American friend and lastly in his apprehension and killing of him, defines his search in terms of the black and white, villain and hero logic of the popular fiction westerns he writes. The moral absolutes this fictional world implies is the world of American popular culture. The film posits both the allure of this culture and its danger for postwar European society. As Holly Martins, the writer of U.S. westerns investigates his friend's disappearance, he literally leaves pillage in his wake. His indiscrete investigations lead to, among other things, the senseless death of the Viennese porter who originally wished to help him with information. When he meets with the Czech actress Anna in the bar at the Casanova Club, he bellows loudly at a group of Russian soldiers as they enter the establishment. Anna, newly divested of her 'western papers' by Major Calloway and the Russian authorities in Vienna, urgently begs Martins to be quiet. Here Martins' actions threaten Anna with exposure to the Russians. The influence of American popular culture as Martins represents it in his search for his friend has all the characteristics of spreading disease, all the more as Martins' apparent cluelessness can almost be framed as a type of 'natural' or neutral force that infects and destroys the things it touches in the name of moral rectitude (Scholz, *From Fidelity to History* 28-53).

It is the character of Anna who represents the European view of things in the film. She calls Martins on characteristics he shares with his friend Harry: a penchant for disowning the destructive consequences of his own values and beliefs without the ability to respect the otherness of the other. Martins has a tendency to see the world through the black and white constructions of his own fiction rather than through the grey lens of postwar reality. The spread of such 'fiction' is akin to the spread of disease, and, in the eyes of Anna Schmidt in particular, an illness she wishes not to contract. The two characters who claim to like Holly Martins' 'wild west' stories, Calloway's assistant Sargent Paine and Baron Kurtz, the co-organizer (with Lime) of the penicillin scheme, are fated to death or imprisonment at the end. Sargent Paine, one of the most sympathetic European characters in the film, dies of a gunshot wound inflicted by Harry Lime in the chase through the Vienna sewers. The shootout that closes the film mirrors a central feature of western popular fiction and confirms its deadly nature for European audiences.

Holly Martins ultimately threatens to contaminate Europe irrevocably by falling in love with Anna. Anna Schmidt chooses to remain aloof of the moral absolutes that Holly's fictional world implies—her resistance to him reveals the film's consistent emphasis on 'resistance to contamination' even to the point where it jeopardizes the implications of its own formula. While Holly Martins will continue to view himself in the role of her rescuer to the very end, the conclusion of the film unmistakably quarantines Holly into a separate world where he can no longer exercise influence over Anna. In the final scene in the Vienna Central Cemetery, the space and distance required to resist exposure to Martins are visually unambiguous. Holly remains at a distance, Anna walks past Holly without eye contact, without an exchange of words.

Anna's rejection of the American Holly Martins also very much reflected the stance of the British and European producers of the film: Carol Reed, author Graham Greene and producer Alexander Korda vis-à-vis the American producer David O. Selznick. Selznick's wish to control the plot development of the film to conform to the romantic melodrama mode, like Martins' pulp western fiction, jeopardized the creative goals of the films production team: to entertain audiences by establishing a European view on the American influence in Europe. There was no real room for constructive compromise between equal parties, as the postwar parties were entirely unequal. Rather, distance and space needed to be established. Quarantining

Europe from the influence of U.S. Cold War culture was a prerequisite for creative autonomy and national health.

* * *

How then to publicize a film that sought to question Cold War absolutes within an increasingly hardening Cold War context? In Greene's original story *The Third Man* and indeed, even in the revised story published after the film's release, the characters of Holly Martins (Rollo Martins in the book) and Harry Lime are first Canadian, then British nationals. The casting of two well-known and popular American actors in the roles of villain and anti-hero in the film created an implied link between the characters' nationality and their functions in the plot, a link that was not lost on David Selznick. In a memo to his 'foreign secretary' Betty Goldsmith, dated October 16, 1948, he wrote:

> I certainly am going to insist upon certain basic things on which I spent many, many long hours of wrangling in order to get Reed's and Greene's agreement; thus, for instance, the script is written as though England were the sole occupying power in Vienna, with some Russians vaguely in the distance; with an occasional Frenchman wandering around; and with, most important from the standpoint of this criticism, the only American being an occasional soldier who apparently is merely part of the British occupying force, plus the heavy (Lime), plus the hero…and just to make matters worse, the American hero apparently is completely subject to the orders and instructions of the British authorities, and behaves as if there were no Americans whatsoever among the occupying powers, nor any American authority, and indeed as far as this picture is concerned, there is none. It would be little short of disgraceful on our part as Americans if we tolerated this nonsensical handling of the four power occupation of Vienna…I went through this at the greatest length…with Reed and Greene and come hell or high water, I simply will not stand for it in its present form. (Selznick 446)

From the United States Selznick generated such memos, insisting that the negative implications of U.S. actors playing ambiguous characters in an occupied European city should be offset with an emphasis upon the positive role of the Americans in postwar Europe and their role as the new arbiters of freedom and democracy. Reed and Greene, as they claimed, ignored these memos and refused to allow any of Selznick's advice to shape the end product. None of Selznick's suggestions, to give the Americans a greater role in occupied Vienna, to glamorize the lead actress or to rename the film *Night in Vienna* instead of *The Third Man,* became a part of the final film.

* * *

In the following discussion I would like to present two little known on location publicity stills for *The Third Man* that conform to Selznick's agenda to give Americans more visual presence in Vienna. These stills differed sharply from those that focused upon the (apolitical) entertainment aspects of the film emphasized by the British production team: suspense—for example, Harry Lime in sinister pose—or pathos—Holly Martins gazing longingly at the emotionally inaccessible Anna Schmidt.

In Figure 1 we see the conception of the American influence as the U.S. producer Selznick would have envisioned it.[1] Joseph Cotten, one of the lead actors contributed to the production by Selznick Studios, passes out C.A.R.E. packages to a grateful and happy group of Viennese children and their parents. C.A.R.E., which originally stood for "Cooperative for American Remittances to Europe" was a consortium of private charity organizations in the United States. Its goal was to deliver food aid to victims of war in Europe (Morris 5-8). The original C.A.R.E. packages were army rations privately purchased and mailed to specific individuals; however, by 1948, the packages began to be generally and generically distributed, for example "to a hungry person in Europe". Thus, the C.A.R.E. program expanded its mandate and became identified with broad relief efforts worldwide (C.A.R.E. (relief agency).

The packages in the still contained an assortment of goods, basic nutritional infrastructure for the preparation of meals such as flour and rice (it's

[1] To view Fig.1, see https://www.google.com/search?tbm=bks&q=From+Fidelity+to+History, 37.

Uncle Ben's rice in the package Cotten is distributing) but also luxury items such as raisins and chocolate, which would certainly explain the smiling faces of the children. These goods are displayed in a row behind the figures on the still. The box contained thirty pounds in all, enough, according to the original function of the C.A.R.E. package as "U.S. army rations packs" to provide one complete meal for ten soldiers (C.A.R.E. [relief agency]). In Vienna in 1948, the caption of the C.A.R.E. still states: the "food parcels" were distributed to "needy Austrian children" (Caption Text Figure 1).

To link the postwar C.A.R.E. campaign in Austria to *The Third Man* was clearly an attempt- more likely initiated by Selznick than by Carol Reed and Alexander Korda-the British producers- to associate the production with "the overwhelming achievements of the U.S. economic system" and thus to highlight the connection between "philanthropic relief and U.S. foreign policy goals" (Wagnleitner 52). Ironically, this image contrasts starkly with the role the American characters in the film would actually play: Holly Martins, the writer, offers not economic aid to Viennese children but hack Western fiction and his ostensibly dead friend, Harry Lime, offers not food and medicine but poison, infection, disease and corruption as represented by the racket Harry Lime runs in the film: selling diluted penicillin to military hospitals on the black market.

As it turned out, this C.A.R.E. still with Joseph Cotten would not circulate widely (if at all) in German-speaking countries. While it is possible that the stark contrast between the image of benevolence in the still and the agenda of black market corruption in the film might have led to preventing this still from entering circulation in Europe, a more likely reason for its absence might well be explained by Austrian and European ambivalence at being depicted as dependent on American economic aid. As American government officials were aware, Europeans could find "American economic aid psychologically galling" (Bischof 165). So it is not surprising that much of the publicity for *The Third Man* that actually did circulate in Austria and Germany preferred, for example, to focus on the centrality of German-speaking actors and actresses in the production (Scholz, *From Fidelity to History* 31-33), or other aspects that highlighted the significance of the European and, in Austria, the Austrian aspects of the film: its setting, Vienna and the Austrian origins of its players.

Another intriguing U.S.-centered publicity still for *The Third Man* offers a more ambiguous reading of the relationship between the U.S. and Austria

(Figure 2).[2] The still's caption indicates that we are looking at "Orson Welles with a policeman in front of the Parliament building in Vienna" (Caption Text Figure 2). However, both are dressed very much like their characters in the film. Therefore, they are visually representing their characters as well as 'themselves.' The two figures are standing in front of the Vienna Parliament by the Pallas-Athena fountain. The dramatic black and white contrast between the newly re-democratized Parliament building (it had been the seat of the Vienna Reichsgau during the Nazi occupation of Austria between 1938 and 1945) (Parliamentsgebäude [Wien]) and the dark figures standing before it certainly invokes the visual aesthetics of *The Third Man*. Yet here it is not the ruins of Vienna, or its postwar economic desperation that are emphasized but rather its political institutions and its high cultural legacy. The statue of the Goddess of Wisdom that towers above the head of the arch criminal Harry Lime and the American superstar Orson Welles are facing in exactly opposing directions, yet visually they compose one figure. Thus, on one level, this image of the smiling cynic blending seamlessly into the 'Goddess of Wisdom' evokes the opposing philosophies of democracy and anti-democracy as Lime had articulated them in his cuckoo clock-speech.

If we are looking at the American actor Orson Welles here, as the caption suggests, then the still could imply a both/and solution to the problem of democracy and culture. American culture will now function to promote both democratic institutions and to protect the high cultural legacy of the city of Vienna. It contradicts Lime's philosophical stance that war and terror beget high culture by visually situating the dramatic sculpture of the Goddess of Wisdom, an embodiment of high culture, as emerging from the figure of the American Welles. Now that the Nazis have been purged from the Parliament, the Austrian political system, with the help of America, can function to bring democracy and high culture together.

On the other hand, more ominously, if we are looking at the character of Harry Lime chatting with the Austrian policeman (he is very likely a film extra as well), the still would suggest collusion between the American criminal and the Austrian law in 'reality.' In contrast, the film depicts the police pursuing the criminal Lime through the sewers of Vienna. Thus the still could be read as a type of pact with the devil—Athena's facing away from these two suggests ambivalence and indeed, disapproval of their friendship.

Like the explicitly political C.A.R.E. package still that depicted the

---

[2] To view Fig. 2 see https://www.google.com/search?tbm=bks&q=From+Fidelity+to+History, 43.

average Viennese citizens (women and children) as economic beneficiaries of U.S. Cold War policy, this politically ambiguous depiction of Austrian high culture in the form of Athena, the Goddess of Wisdom, in front of the Vienna Parliament emerging out of and towering above the American black market penicillin swindler and advocate of fascism, Harry Lime, on the one hand, or the American actor Orson Welles on the other, did not circulate widely, I would argue, because it did not contain the elements that would make the film *The Third Man* appealing to Austrian audiences.

* * *

The critical response to *The Third Man* in Austria and Germany offers insights into why the politicized publicity stills did not enjoy a wide circulation, if any at all. In an article in the German newspaper *Die Zeit* entitled "Wien und der 'Dritte Mann'" ("Vienna and *The Third Man*") published in 1950 from Vienna, the question was raised why a film that depicted the city of Vienna and its many war ruins in such an "uncompassionate" ("mitleidslos") way could be so popular with Austrians:[3]

> The film has the uncanny effect that it gives the experiences of the time of hunger, insecurity and the absolute domination of the allied military police a realistic character. Until now these were just nightmares: the experiences of that brief, terrible phase are stored between thick walls of completely different memories. They are atypical and unbelievable. The testimony of the foreigner, who has access to the most impressive filmic means, thus feels like an important confirmation. "Yes, that's exactly the way it was" is heard everywhere [here]. It is in this moment that the events seem to become a part of the past, for the nightmares were never completely over. It was a childish illusion to say "I don't want to remember." The

[3] My evidence clearly suggests that *The Third Man* was as popular in Austria as it was in other European countries and the United States; see "Wien und der dritte Mann" as well as "Filme der Woche: Der Dritte Mann". For a recently widely circulated discussion in the British newspaper *The Guardian* arguing the opposite, see Cook (2006). For a more detailed analysis of the critical response to the depiction of Vienna in the film see Scholz, *From Fidelity to History* 42-43.

> memory was a part of the self, after all, and did not require the will to call it forth ([H.M.W.] 3).[4]

According to H.M.W., the author of "Vienna and *the Third Man*", a particular emotional dynamic shaped the film's overall effect on Austrian audiences. The film seemed to function as a kind of immediate 'Vergangenheitsbewältigung' (coming to terms with the past), that is, a means of coping with the harsh memories of the war years and indeed, immediate postwar years. In this sense, it could be argued that *The Third Man* functioned in Austria much as some of the more successful 'Trümmerfilme' (rubble films) functioned in postwar Germany: as a way to give meaning to the experiences of war and postwar trauma borne of hunger, deprivation, need, and military occupation (Svetov 15-16). Significantly, the emphasis would be placed on the status of personal victimhood and not on responsibility for aggressive national politics, in the case of Germany (Shandley 20-76), or, in the case of Austria, collaboration during the Nazi occupation (Löffler 175-93, 203-15).

Figure 3 shows a typical on location- still from the film that can conceivably be read as the above review suggests.[5] It depicts the American Holly Martins (Joseph Cotten). He's had a few drinks too many, and he's just seen his old friend Harry Lime—a friend he believed dead—disappear somewhere on the square 'Am Hof' in post-WWII Vienna. He is torn between doubts over his own sanity, unrequited love for his friend's Czech girlfriend Anna, relief that his friend may still be alive, and near certainty that Harry is mixed up in a vicious black market racket. The darkness and mysterious aura of the Vienna square reinforces the haunted expression on Holly's face. His predicament—that of an enterprising but unwelcome

---

[4] All subsequent English translations from the German are my own. Orig. German text: „Zunächst hat der Film die verblüffende Wirkung, daß die Erlebnisse aus der Zeit des Hungers, der Unsicherheit und der absoluten Herrschaft der allierten Militärpolizei Wirklichkeitscharakter erhalten. Bisher waren sie noch immer so etwas wie böse Angstträume; die Erlebnisse jener kurzen, schrecklichen Phase lagern ja in mächtigen Schichten gänzlich anderer Erinnerungen, sie sind atypisch, unglaubwürdig. Die fremde Zeugenaussage, der die eindrucksvollsten filmischen Mittel zur Verfügung standen, wirkt daher wie eine wichtige Bestätigung. „Ja, so war es…genau so" hört man immer wieder sagen, und in diesem Augenblick scheinen die Ereignisse erst in die Vergangenheit zu sinken. Denn die bösen Träume waren ja nie ganz ausgeträumt, es war eine kindliche Täuschung, wenn man sagte: „Ich will mich an all das gar nicht erinnern." Die Reminiszenz war doch ein Teil des „Ich", bedurfte also keinesfalls einer Ermunterung durch den Willen."

[5] To view Fig. 3, see http://berghahnbooks.com/blog/will-the-real-vienna-please-stand-up

American pulp fiction writer stumbling through the labyrinth of postwar Europe—is inextricably linked with the city where he finds himself.

As the *Zeit* article suggested, an important aspect of this postwar 'reality' had to do with the marked ambivalence of Europeans toward the influence and presence of American military and popular culture. This quality is reflected, ironically, in the American Holly Martin's expression as he ponders whether he should not catch the next plane out of Vienna before he finds out more than he wants to know. His face, framed by the dark Vienna square, mirrors his own disappointed expectations as well as those of European and Austrian audiences, who were both mesmerized by and deeply suspicious of America's role in postwar Europe (Scholz, "Will the Real Vienna").

If a large portion of Austrian and German audiences appreciated *The Third Man*'s attempt to visualize the scenario of suffering and victimization of the immediate postwar years, they were also more than happy with the unhappy end in *The Third Man*. No doubt the most famous on location-image of *The Third Man* is Anna Schmidt's walk past Holly Martins after Lime's burial in the Vienna Central Cemetery. This melancholy scene was discussed with great enthusiasm by Alex Natan in a review of *The Third Man*, also from *Die Zeit*. He writes:

> The "third man" has been buried. His lover walks along a long, tree-lined lane towards the camera [...] Leaning on the side is the American, who has fallen in love with the woman and who believes he can buy her with C.A.R.E. packages[6] [...] She doesn't see the American, she walks past him, a European woman, like millions of other continental women, who still have their pride, their feminine dignity—that is not a "happy end," it isn't an end at all. It's life (reality). The greatness of "The Third Man" is based on the fact that it has become a mirror of continental life. Unforgettable.[7] (Natan)

---

[6] This provocative comment suggests that the C.A.R.E. package publicity still may have been known to the reviewer; unfortunately, I have no direct evidence for this yet.

[7] Orig. German: "Der ‚Dritte Mann' ist beerdigt worden. Seine Geliebte geht eine lange Friedhofsallee auf die Kamera zu [...] Am Wege lehnt der Amerikaner, der sich in die Frau verliebt hat und sie durch Carepakete kaufen zu können glaubt [...] Sie sieht den Amerikaner nicht, sie geht an ihm vorüber, eine europäische Frau, wie sie auf unseren Kontinent zu Millionen leben, die noch ihren Stolz, ihre weibliche Würde haben—das ist kein „Happy End", das ist überhaupt kein Ende, das ist Leben. Die Größe des Third Man beruht in der Tatsache, dass er zum Spiegel kontinentalen Lebens geworden ist. Unvergesslich."

This evaluation suggests that audiences from the early fifties preferred seeing Europe associated with a woman who rejects an American than women who accept his proffered C.A.R.E. packages.

The notion that *The Third Man* 'mirrored' life in Vienna in the immediate postwar period is reinforced by the critic D.G., writing in the left-leaning social-democratic (SPÖ) Austrian newspaper *Arbeiter-Zeitung* in 1950, and this despite its lack of 'factual accuracy':

> The film's plotting is [...] not without its flaws, especially for the Viennese viewer who is familiar [with the four power occupation]. But is this so important? *The Third Man* isn't supposed to be a documentary film in the sense of an historically accurate chronicle. The film wants to capture a moment of a time gone awry, in a city that mirrored the entire insanity of this time—the peculiar, depressing atmosphere of occupation and insecurity, of poverty and postwar immorality. All this is captured masterfully.[8] ([D.G.] 7)

Those dimensions of the film defined as real are all tied to the conception of the occupation as essentially negative and oppressive in character. By implication, the U.S. dimension of that same occupation, rather than being distinguished as positive, as in the C.A.R.E. still, is instead a part of the nightmare of the film's 'reality': "of occupation and insecurity, of poverty and postwar immorality" (D.G. 7).

* * *

What do we make of the contemporary reception of the film in Austria and Germany? If we return to the image of Joseph Cotten distributing C.A.R.E. packages and compare it to the final shot of *The Third Man* we can see that the implications of these very different images of the U.S./Austrian relation-

[8] Orig. German text: "Die reine Handlung des Films ist [...] vor allem für den Wiener der sich auskennt, nicht ganz hieb-und stichfest. Aber kommt es darauf an? Der dritte Mann soll ja kein Dokumentarfilm im Sinne einer geschichtlich exakten Chronik sein. Er will einen Ausschnitt aus der aus den Fugen gegangenen Zeit zeigen, in einer Stadt in der sich die ganze Verrücktheit dieser Zeit widerspiegelt, mit der eigentümlichen, bedrückenden Atmosphäre von Besetzung und Unsicherheit, von Not und Nachkriegsunmoral. Und das ist meisterhaft gelungen" (D.G. 7).

ship have both a negative and a positive function. Negatively, British (and by extension, European) culture seeking to separate or quarantine itself from U.S. culture implies a form of anti-Americanism, a traditional perspective on the U.S. seen through the lens of postwar Europe: the elitist opposition between high culture (represented by Europe) and popular or low culture, represented by the U.S. Yet the film's stance on the question of seeing the U.S. and Europe (and by extension, Austria) as different cultures with different agendas is not a rejection of the influence of American culture as such. Rather, it is a rejection of the Cold War logic that stipulated that the influence of American culture in Europe represented an unambiguous moral good, a disinterested humanitarianism with no pretensions to power and influence.

The Third Man as postwar thriller sought to question this inflated conception of postwar America by cordoning off an alternative European realm as an antidote to the Cold War's opposition between East and West. This agenda, however, conflicted with the U.S. producer David Selznick's goals for the film. In the film publicity stills discussed in this essay, the overall Cold War framework situated the United States as the rescuer (from war, hunger, fascism, communism) of Europe rather than as a victorious occupying force. This was not a message Austrian or German viewers were interested in. For them, the appeal of the film lay in a creative use of Austrian urban space, theatrical talent and music that spoke to a collective sense of victimization borne of war and its aftermath. And because this was done without pontificating about the Cold War or in any way raising questions of war responsibility or complicity with criminal actions during the war—it was celebrated as an aesthetically brilliant 'mirror' of postwar 'reality'—and is to this day.

WORKS CITED

Behlmer, Rudy, ed. *Memo from: David O. Selznick*. New York: Avon, 1972.

Bischof, Günter. "Two Sides of the Coin: The Americanization of Austria and Austrian Anti-Americanism." Ed. Alexander Stephan. *The Americanization of Europe: Culture, Diplomacy, and Anti-Americanism after 1945*. New York and Oxford: Berghahn, 2006: 147-184.

Caption Text Figure 1: Publicity Still [RF2/Pub/63A]: "Joseph Cotten handing out food parcels to needy Austrian children..." David O. Selznick Collection. Harry Ransom Center, U of Texas at Austin.

Caption Text Figure 2: Publicity Still [RF2/Pub/65]: "Orson Welles mit einem Polizisten vor dem Parliamentsgebäude in Wien." Deutsche Kinemathek, Berlin.

C.A.R.E. (relief agency). *Wikipedia: the free Encyclopedia.* http://en.wikipedia.org/w/index.php?title=C.A.R.E._(relief_agency)&oldid=631103997. Accessed 24 Oct. 2014.

Cook, William. "*The Third Man*'s View of Vienna." *The Guardian* (8 Dec. 2006). www.theguardiancom/film/2006/dec/08/3

D.G. "Film der Woche: *Der Dritte Mann.*" *Arbeiter-Zeitung* (Wien). 12.03.1950: 7. arbeiter-zeitung.at

Greene, Graham. *The Third Man/The Fallen Idol.* Harmondsworth: Penguin Books in assoc. with William Heinemann, 1976.

H.M.W. "Wien und der 'dritte Mann'" *Die Zeit* 13.April 1950: 3. www.zeit.de/1950/15/wien-und-der-dritte-mann.

Löffler, Sigrid. *Kritiken, Portraits, Glossen.* Wien: Franz Deuticke Verlagsgesellschaft mbH, 1995.

Morris, David. *A Gift From America: The First 50 Years of C.A.R.E..* Atlanta, Georgia: Longstreet P, 1996.

Natan, Alex. "Der dritte Mann." *Die Zeit* 12.01.1950.

Parliamentsgebäude (Wien). *Wikipedia: Die freie Enzyklopedie.* http://de.wikipedia.org/wiki/Parlamentsgeb%C3%A4ude_(Wien). Accessed 1 Jan. 2014.

Philanthropy-Growing Influence. *Encyclopedia of the New American Nation* (online). http://www.americanforeignrelations.com/O-W/Philanthropy-Growing-influence.html. Accessed 20 Oct. 2016.

Scholz, Anne-Marie. *From Fidelity to History: Film Adaptations as Cultural Events In the Twentieth Century.* New York and Oxford: Berghahn, 2013.

"Will the Real Vienna Please Stand Up?"posted 13.05.2013, Berghahn Books Blog. http://berghahnbooks.com/blog/will-the-real-vienna-please-stand-up. Accessed 29 July 2013.

Selznick, David O. Memo to Betty Goldsmith, 16.10.1948. in Behlmer, Rudy, ed. *Memo from: David O. Selznick*: 446.

Shadowing the Third Man. Dir. Frederick Baker. British Broadcasting, Media Europe, et al., 2004.

The Third Man. Wikipedia: the Free Encyclopedia. http://en.wikipedia.org/w/index.php?title=The_Third_Man&oldid=630860612 Accessed 21 Oct. 2014.

Shandley, Robert R. *Trümmerfilme: Das deutsche Kino der Nachkriegszeit.* Berlin: Parthas Verlag, 2010. Trans. Axel Meier.Originalaus: *Rubble Films: German Cinema in the Shadow of the Third Reich.* Temple UP, 2001.

Svetov, Marc. "Rubble Noir: A Postwar Vision of the Vanquished." *Noir City*, Summer 2014, filmnoirfoundation.org: 15-24.

Wagnleitner, Reinhold. *Coca-colonization and the Cold War: The Cultural Mission of the United States in Austria after the Second World War*. Chapel Hill and London: U of North Carolina P, 1994.

MODERNIST DESTRUCTION AND ROMANTIC REDEMPTION: CULTURAL TRANSLATIONS IN *LETTER FROM AN UNKNOWN WOMAN*

YUVAL LUBIN

Texts can be said to be born from the cultural sentiment of the time. Those dialogues and modes of thought which dominate the consciousness of society are very often exemplified in the texts of that era. At the same time, the culture of adaptation which exists in cinema can often emphasize those very cultural sentiments. Adapted texts can differ from their source by promoting different ideologies. As a result, the comparison of representations in such adapted texts and their sources can be used to exemplify the different ideologies the texts embody.

Such is the case with *Letter from an Unknown Woman*. In 1922 Stefan Zweig published his short novella *A Letter from an Unknown Woman*. The novella presents a tragic relationship: the woman continually obsesses over R. at the cost of her social standing and dignity, while he repeatedly forgets her. [39] In 1948, Max Ophüls adapted the novella to a film by the same name. The adaptation made several changes to the novella, including alterations to the plot and the characters. Though the film still follows a story similar to that of the novella, the changes made are fundamental, promoting a more positive view of events and essentially changing the ideas that are the driving force of the novella.

In inspecting these changes, one sees that they are cultural in nature. The translation of the novella into film shifts the themes and ideals underlying the narrative. As such the film transforms the novella from a text that inspects Austrian and European modernist sentiments to a romantic text emblematic of American culture at the moment of its adaptation.

The novella depicts a bleak view of modern life. It deals with the destruction of the self through loss of identity, and the dwindling vitality of existence that is incorporated into art. Throughout the novella, the woman loses everything that identifies her, until she finally becomes the cultural back-

[1] In this analysis of the text, I will refer to the protagonist of the novella as "the woman" and her love interest as 'R.' as he appears in the novella (Zweig 423). Their film counterparts are named Liza and Brand, respectively.

ground noise to R.'s existence. The way in which the novella dismantles the woman represents the modern notions of loss of the individual's meaning. This is in sharp contrast to the American reinterpretation of the story. Instead of the dark and pessimistic vision suggested in the novella, the film espouses an empowering conception of the individual. The film portrays the woman, Liza, as an expressly individual character, differentiated from the world around her and possessing an immensely powerful will. Her affair with Brand, a promiscuous pianist with whom she falls in love as a child, pushes Liza to act in ways that would shape reality to her desire. Through Liza the film offers an optimistic view of the world, where individuals can affect their will on the world and thus give it meaning.

While following the same plotline, the novella and the adaptation depict drastically different and converse concepts of the individual. Certain elements in the two texts offer a clear view of how the pessimistic novella is translated into the optimistic film: the representation of culture, the composition of actions and of characters, and ultimately the construction of the final scene. The representations of culture establish the character of the woman as either strong-willed and individualistic or self-effacing. The composition of characters and actions embodies the texts' conception of the narrative, and thus the perception of time as either progressing or fragmented. Finally, the romantic American film ends with the redemption of both of its main characters, while the modernist Austrian novella completely dismantles the idea of human identity and establishes life as being constructed on the ruins of history and individuality. By examining the contrasting elements between the film and the novella, this chapter analyzes the romantic ideology of individualism in the film and its difference from the modernist notion of individual decline in the novella.

Since the subject of this chapter is the cultural translation of Austrian sentiments into American ideas, it seems fitting to begin by inspecting the representation of Austrian culture as it is depicted in the film.

The film is abundant with representations of Austrian culture. The events of the story take place in Vienna and Linz, and the film does much to foreground the Austrian location of the film. Culture is used in the film to juxtapose Liza and the society that surrounds her. Conveying Liza as different from her surroundings allows the film to define her as an individual, which amplifies her power to affect reality through her will.

The first and most apparent representation of the film's Austrian setting is the use of accents. Though most characters do not have distinctly European accents, several minor characters use conspicuous Austrian accents. Such is the case with the moving laborers at the beginning of the film who move Brand's possessions into his new apartment. Due to their exaggerated nature the purpose of the accents appears not be verisimilitude, but rather comedy. The menials exchange silly jokes while working, giving their characters comedic undertones. The accents are used to extenuate the comedy and mark the characters as amusing.

This use of accents in this manner foregrounds the difference between Liza and these characters, emphasizing the difference between her and the characters surrounding her. The characters' affected accents makes them unrelatable figures, foreign male working-class caricatures. The film juxtaposes this to Liza's overwhelming narration which is not hindered by a European accent. As a result, the comedic characters help to elevate Liza's first encounter with Brand, empowering its significance. The use of the comedic accents presents her as the only real fully-developed character in the scene. Through this colocation, Liza is presented as a unique individual compared with those around her, capable of imbuing the events depicted with meaning and possessing a personal, reflexive view of the world. The proliferation of Austrian accents foregrounds her voice and emphasizes the significance of her narrative in comparison with the lesser dialogues that inhabit the scene as well as the film.

Thus culture is used to define Liza as an individual, contrasted with the society around her. In her article on the film, Laura Mulvey suggests that culture is represented in the film as a form of oppression, limiting Liza's social abilities and attempting to force her to conform to certain modes of action that are contrary to her will (7). However, I find that it is Liza's opposition to these attempts at suppression that define her character and the film. Liza's oppression by culture and her rebellion are best depicted in her affair with the young soldier in Linz.

The abundant use of military imagery in the Linz scenes again underlines the setting's Austrian qualities, conveying Austrian culture through the depiction of obviously Austrian military uniforms and the positive social standing of officers in bourgeois society. As with the accents, the depiction of Austrian culture does much to define Liza as an individual. Liza's relationship with the soldier in Linz portrays society's coercion of Liza to conform, and her definition through opposition to the same society. The subject takes form in the film in the form of Liza's Linz suitor. In Linz Liza, at the prompting of her parents, engages in a relationship with a soldier in the army. The cultural elements of the relationship are foregrounded by the film and represent the oppressive force that attempts to control Liza.

The depiction of Liza's suitor as a soldier firmly positions the interaction within a cultural context, implying both the idea of suitable class-coupling and the limiting of Liza's social independence. According to Mulvey, the army is a garrison of male social power which excludes women from social affect (10). From this, marriage to the soldier would position Liza within a class structure, giving her a "place in society" while depriving her of the ability to affect her will on the world. Furthermore, we see that the actual interaction is also limited by cultural constraints. The Linz scenes begin with Liza's mother attempting to structure Liza's behavior, instructing her on how to act during the interactions with the suitor. The positioning of these instructions at the beginning of the scene foregrounds the limiting nature of the relationship. This conveys the controlling nature of culture in the relationship between Liza and the soldier. Society operates in the film as an oppressive power that attempts to define Liza according to social conventions, depicted in representations of Austrian culture.

Nevertheless, Liza is not defined by the cultural constraints imposed upon women, but rather by her opposition to these cultural structures. In these Linz scenes, Liza is shown to have two interactions with the intended lieutenant. During both encounters Liza speaks but very little, however in the first encounter she contributes very little to the interaction and mostly agrees with the soldier. During the second encounter Liza maintains a similar attitude until she divulges her secret, if currently unreal, affair with Brand. In the first instance Liza's curt speech is a product of her resistance to the social obligations she is under. She is defined here by her involuntary participation in the courtship game. This culminates in the following scene, where Liza opposes social dictums directly. She breaks of the engagement and claims to be engaged without her parents' consent. In doing so, Liza is repositioned as external to the traditional social order depicted in Linz. By disinclining to take part in her parents' marriage plans and the culturally structured engagement process, Liza is becomes a figure for the oppressed sentiments and values stifled by the current social dogma.

Liza's overwhelming will is further exemplified by her transition back to Vienna. Though in the novella her move is explained as being assisted by her family, the question of how she moved back and found a job, as well as her relationship with her family after the events in Linz, are omitted (Zweig 438). Rather, the transition to Vienna is presented in a single line that does not reference any difficulties in moving at all (Ophüls). By representing her departure in this manner, the film conveys Liza's will as being overwhelming. She is able to take extreme actions with ease, severing ties with her family and beginning a new life in a city on her own by the sheer power of her resolve. Liza bends the world to her wishes, creating the reality she wants despite any possible hindrances: a reality where she can see Brand.

In this manner Liza is defined by being opposed to those around her, who are characterized by their strong and obvious relations to Austrian culture. She is figured as an individual by her contrast with the caricatures of the working men and as an affecting figure by her opposition to class restrictions. Her rejection of bourgeois society and assertion of will define her as a romantic figure: one who possesses an encompassing willpower that can alter reality and glorifies the power of the individual person.

However, these unique elements which define the character of Liza in the movie seem to be completely alien when approaching its Austrian source material, in which the character of the woman in the story tends towards self-effacement rather than assertion. Zweig's heroine categorically limits and marginalize her effect on her surroundings. This is apparent foremost in the representation of the parallel events in the novella.

As in the film, the unnamed woman of the novella rejects society and avoids social interaction. Yet, instead of the heroic opposition depicted in the film, the woman in the novella retreats completely from any social interaction. This is represented by a list of social activities which the woman refuses, culminating in her statement, "I hardly went out at all" (Zweig 437). This catalogue of continuous cancellation of inter-personal interaction does not convey self-asserting opposition as in the film, but rather a self-effacing mentality. The woman purposefully avoids having any effect on those around her, or even developing as an individual.

Her failure to generate any personal growth is emphatically apparent by her declaration that she did not learn to know more than ten streets in her two years in Innsbruck (Zweig 437). Her rejection of such cursory knowledge of her surroundings conveys her avoidance of personal, experiential growth. In her time in Innsbruck she did not generate a single meaningful personal experience that defined her character. moreover, she states that during her time there, her actions almost completely consisted of remembering the events of her relation to her lover in Vienna: "I stayed at home alone for hours, days, doing nothing but thinking of you again and again, always reviving my hundred little memories of you, every time I met you, every time I waited for you, staging those little incidents in my mind as if in a theatre" (437).

The complete immersion presented in this sentence represents the intellectual stasis the woman relegates herself to. She does not develop any new mental convictions or expand her mind in any way, but rather utterly shuts herself within the confines of her already-established memories. The woman's choice of social and mental stasis is self-effacing in nature. She actively aborts any development in her self-conception. Thus, she sustains her existing identity instead of expanding it through synthesis of new experiences and thoughts. In this manner, the woman nullifies her own existence, preventing development in her identity by removing herself from reality and its altering effects.

One could argue that though effacing herself in relation to society, the woman asserts individuality through her investment in her love towards R. Still, even in her love for R., the woman is represented as self-effacing. Inspecting the language the woman uses when discussing her love, the concept of will is utterly subverted. When describing her attempt to see R. before leaving for Innsbruck with her family, the woman says, "I did not so much walk: it was more as if, with my stiff legs and trembling joints I was magnetically attracted to your door" (435). The phrase invokes the image of the woman as an automaton, incapable of volition and overtaken by her emotions. It is not surprising that here the woman only crosses a hallway rather than an entire city like her film counterpart. By using this language, the woman relinquishes her agency in her life, deferring to R. and his effect over her. She is a passive figure who conceives of herself as having no control over her actions, and even ceding any authority she has in affecting her life.

Her use of language goes even further, completely denying the woman humanity under the effect of love. Earlier in the novella the woman attributes to herself words such as "slave," "dog" and "creature" (431). The words are expressly degrading and have the connotation of lacking will or control over one's own life. The use of such words shows that the woman dehumanizes herself, forgoing in the process basic human attributes such as position in the world, responsibility over her actions and the right to assert her will.

As a result, a very different figure of the heroine is presented in the novella. She is a figure who actively avoids having any interaction with the world that surrounds her, preventing her ability to affect and be affected by reality. She gives up the right to control her existence, becoming a passive figure that cannot impose upon the world. Her conception as being separate from the present through her lack of agency and obsession with recollection defines her as a modernist character. As such she abandons action in favor of living through reflection. Passivity and self-reflection are common attributes amongst modernist characters. Joyce's modernist epic *Ulysses* centers around two such characters. Both Leopold Bloom and Stephen Dedalus avoid confrontations in such a way that marginalizes themselves. The two of them are displaced from their home, Stephen by his dispute with Mulligan and Bloom due to his wife's affair. Furthermore, Joyce's use of stream of consciousness, marked by a verisimilitude to unfiltered thoughts, convey how both characters interpret their experiences through reference and analysis. Such is also the case with T. S. Eliot's narrating voice in *The Wasteland.* This ambitious poem stiches together fragments of human culture, including segments from the bible, Mallarme and Greek mythology in an attempt to present some form of encompassing image. The incongruous elements are presented out of context and become subjects of reflection external to their original texts. At the same time the fragmentation of the text defines it as a construction of ruins which relinquishes the concept of being like the texts it refers to. Though Zweig's woman is not quite as symbolically intricate as the previous examples, her ability to annihilate her agency encapsulates this defining element of modernist style.

Thus we have two very distinct and opposing characters. On the one hand, Liza of the film is a romantic figure. Some of Romanticism's most notable characteristics are an intensity of emotion, individuality and recreating reality through projection of emotions. Liza is uniquely individual in the film, capable of acting outside of social norms. These lead her to develop exceptionally intense feelings for brand. Liza projects her desires and emotions onto the outside world, altering and affecting it to suit her desires. On the other, the woman of the novella is a self-effacing character who actively relinquishes her position in the world as both a vehicle of effect and an individual, representing modernist sentiments of the loss of individuality and personal vitality. To go back to Joyce, both Bloom and Stephen suffer during the novel from virility issues, the first sexually while the second artistically. The inability to produce symbolizes loss of vitality with which Joyce contends. Similarly, Eliot's use of fragments and allusions creates a conflict between the narrating voice and the allusions which dramatize the issue of individual voice in the poem. The woman of the novella personifies these elements to an extreme as she nullifies her identity and autonomy in her reflective behavior.

Both film and novella supplement the characterization of the heroines with a composition that supports their perspectives. The texts construct the representation of characters and events in the narrative in such a way that promotes the characters' respective positions. The texts take upon themselves the heroines' worldview and incorporate it into the textual devices they employ. The use of devices such as cinematography and setting the same as textual breaks and ellipsis vindicate the women's perspective in the two works.

The alteration to the character of the woman in the film to an asserting character makes it essential that Liza should matter as an individual. As such, the world in the film must appropriately react to Liza and agree with her wishes. For this reason, the film espouses a belief in a cohesive narrative, a complete image of events in which everything serves a particular purpose and mirrors her desires. It presents a world in which human beings and individuals have intrinsic value and poetic relations.

The film achieves this through the theme of reverberation. In his article about the film, George Wilson describes this essential element of the film: "This device of 'echoing with a variation' is repeated frequently throughout the film, often with the effect of showing the past to be interwoven with the present in ways the characters cannot grasp" (1122). Through the repetition of events and characteristics with alterations, the narrative creates parallelisms which construct the world according to Liza's will. In this manner, the film imbues characters and actions with value and redeems the events portrayed, assigning them meaning.

We see the reverberation of characters in the way Liza and Brand play off one another. In his article "The Paradox of the Unknown Lover: A Reading of *Letter from an Unknown Woman*", Lester H. Hunt claims that both Liza and Brand signify idealistic values (59). Liza and Brand are completely devoted to the idea of love. However, each symbolizes a different aspect of love. Liza is devoted to a romantic mode of love. Her quest to have a relationship with Brand despite obstacles, Brand's flaws, and repeated failures establishes her as an ideal representation of committed and tenacious love. Brand, in contrast, figures a different aspect of love. Mulvey suggests that the film is based in part on the plot of the legend of Don Juan. This analysis of the film helps define Brand as a character committed to the erotic aspect of love: he values the physical act of love and ignores the emotional connection that Liza cherishes. This is shown in the film through his numerous one night stands.

Moreover, Wilson shows that in the final meeting between Liza and Brand, Brand's speech echoes notions that have been associated with Liza's love for him. Yet, appropriated by Brand, the ideas that represented Liza's total commitment and romantic love are transfigured into seduction devices meant to affect Liza (1135). The echoing of Liza's sentiments in this hollow game of seduction positions Brand well within Liza's narrative, defining him in relation to her moral conception of love. He is directly tied to her perception of the world and expresses the way she perceives and interacts with reality, acting as a perverted sounding board for her emotions.

By paralleling Brand to Liza in this manner and subjugating his definition as character to Liza's concept of love, the film creates an intrinsic connection between the two characters: Brand's emotional and moral construction is illuminated by the parallelism to Liza's notion of love. Liza is positioned in the film as a paradigm according to which reality can be analyzed and understood. Her intense pursuit of romantic, emotional love reveals the flaws in Brand's conception of erotic love, and defines his character as self-destructive and morally bankrupt. Thus, the film creates a structure that centers on Liza's individuality as its epistemological basis, turning her reality into an encompassing narrative.

In addition, the entire film apparatus uses reverberations to show the relation between what normally would be disconnected events. This is done in order to give the characters a frame that imbues their actions with meaning. Reverberations of framing in certain scenes and echoing of specific camera shots give purpose to actions and unite the life of Liza into a single, comprehensible image.

One such occasion is the scene after Liza comes back from the train to see Brand before going to Linz. Liza looks down from the staircase at Brand coming home with an unnamed woman, his sexual partner for the night. The shot is framed from an extreme perspective that mimics Liza's view of the scene. The camera is positioned conspicuously high, and Brand and his companion are blocked for a long section of the shot. This extreme perceptive and its correspondence to Liza's perspective symbolize her external position to Brand's life. Furthermore, the blocked view conveys Liza's blindness to Brand's flaws, as well as the separation between them.

This striking composition of the shot returns in a later scene. In this scene, Liza returns with Brand to his apartment after a night out in the first of their two romantic interactions in the film. The return to the aforementioned perspective echoes the themes conveyed in the first iteration. However in this recurrence, Liza is apparently positioned within Brand's life; despite this, the repetition of the perspective identifies her as merely a one night stand, identical to the unknown woman from the earlier scene. According to her own conception of love, Liza is still as external to Brand's life as in the first instance. Her blocked view is also echoed, conveying her blindness in the scene to the true nature of their encounter. It is not the fruition of her longing for a committed relationship with him, but only another chapter in Brand's game of sex.

By echoing the themes of the first scene in the second scene, the film creates a mode of progression in the life of Liza. The film contracts a narrative of discovery: over the course of the film, Liza realizes her position inside Brand's cycle of lovers. By thus presenting the actions in the film, Liza's life is imbued with inherent logic that gives purpose to her actions. Each event in her life is both a product of past events and related to future events. In this manner, Liza's life is turned into a united cohesive narrative in which her actions are purposeful, advancing towards her discovery of Brand's true nature. This affirms her individuality as meaningful; it produces knowledge and unites into a cohesive narrative which has inner relations that illuminate the occurrences in her life.

The novella is not as forgiving as the film in its composition of the story. Unlike the film, it espouses the notion that life is a series of misfortunes and events that cannot come together to give any meaning. It does so through its disjunction of scenes and its foregrounding of death throughout the narrative.

To understand the novella's position on the nature of life's events, it is necessary to inspect the unknown woman's digressive interludes. At one point, the woman claims that men forget women because the constant changes produced by the passage of time make them into new beings. The only appropriate response, in her view, is to be resigned to that fate in order to understand this truth about reality (441). This assertion by the woman symbolizes the view of extreme temporality: time is divided into spots, instances of perception separated from one another. These instances cannot be connected into a unified experience and must be examined separately.

This can be seen in the woman's positive representation of their first erotic encounter. After describing R.'s charming behavior over the course of the evening, the woman comments on the event: "Ah, you have no idea what a wonderful thing you did in not disappointing my five years of childish expectation" (442). The exclamation at the beginning of the sentence positions the positive emotion conveyed as belonging to the woman narrating the story from the position of her recalling, rather than attributed to the woman at the point of the story presented (in the midst of the encounter). It is important to note that the narrating woman possesses the knowledge of the future and is aware that R.'s charm is a seductive guise. This fact does disappoint the woman from a perspective internal to the narration, as she says that after R. left Vienna "[she] waited in despair" (445). The woman's ability to esteem his charm despite later events is a product of this conception of disconnected time. Their evening together is a singular event that produces the positive emotion and, disconnected from other events, is unalterable in its nature. Like all other events in the novella, it is represented as a self-contained entity who is unaffected by other events.

This idea is embodied within the text by the metaphor of the watch: "I was always looking for you, always in a state of tension, but you felt it as little as the tension of a spring watch that you carry in your pocket, patiently counting and measuring your hours in the dark [...] while you let your quick glance fall on it only once in a million ticking seconds" (432). The woman's experience of time is predicated on her interaction with her beloved. Events are interspersed with dead time, time that does not allow for development or definition by recollectable memory. This is symbolized in the hours measured in the dark, in which time continuously progresses but is not perceived, and as such lacks any purpose. Perception occurs when R. looks at the watch; time is defined by a specific number, "a million ticking seconds." However, the definition of time also removes it from the continuous flow of anonymous time, freezing it as an event in which one is aware of time instead of experiencing its progression. In this manner, events become isolated in time. Being conscious of an event comes at the price of being disconnected from other events, as well as the complete course of temporal progression. As a result, events cannot be combined into a whole, an inclusive meaningful narrative, but rather remain as spots in time, chronological anomalies in which the woman is performing her existential purpose (interacting with R.), but which do not constitute a unified whole.

The motif of death does much in conveying the disconnected nature of time in the novella. Death is constantly in the narrative's foreground, separating episodes and disrupting the narration's flow. The novella does not contain chapters, but instead is sectioned by intervals in the print. After each such interval, narration resumes with the woman writing of the present time and referring either to her imminent death or the death of her child (436, 449, 459). By doing this, the text emphasizes the subject of death, reminding readers of its constant presence in the story and affecting the interpretation of the events represented.

By maintaining the death of the woman and the child as the constant background to the events presented, the text prevents events from becoming a progression of a story. Each segment of the woman's life does not develop into the next but is framed by her death. This, too, allows events to remain rooted in themselves and examined as disconnected points in time, becoming separate images. Each image includes a complete representation of the emotional and poetic content of the event, without constituting the basis of the consecutive event's experience.

Such is the case with the first interval in the text. The section ends with the woman, as a small child, seeing R. returning home with a female companion. This scene denotes the woman's sexual awakening and the end of her innocent love. Two things convey this concept: the woman's comment on her intentions at that moment, and the abrupt ending of the scene. The woman says that when coming out to meet him, "[she does not] know what [she] would have done, such a foolish child as [she] was" (436). The sentence ironically contrasts the adult woman's lack of knowledge with the child's sexual latency, conveying the child's inability to offer herself sexually at that moment in time. Thus the woman's sexual immaturity is established in the scene, only to be shattered a moment later when the child discovers that R. is accompanied by another woman.

The section ends abruptly after the discovery of the other woman. The word "woman" ends the scene, with no further information on the events given. The ellipsis in information is presented as an emotional response to the situation and conveys a trauma experienced by the child. This trauma is further conveyed by the next paragraph which consists of two sentences and ends the section. The immediate ending of the segment symbolizes the traumatic response of the child to being faced with R.'s sexual needs and her relation to them as a possible sexual partner.

After this curt conclusion, the narrative turns to the subject of the death of the woman's child in the opening of the next section. The narrative appears to be overtaken by the subject of the child's death, as no mention is made of the events of the previous segment. This is made apparent by the opening statement of the section, which strongly affects a focus on the present time in the narrative, the time of the child's death, and distracts from the events of the past, conveying a sense of disjunction between the sections. This is further emphasized by the seamless transition between the narration regarding the death of the child and the recounting of the woman's life in Innsbruck. The woman connects her feelings of isolation resulting from the child's death and the isolation she felt in Innsbruck (436-37). The connection between the two subjects intrinsically identifies the death of the child with the new section, which foregrounds the division between the trauma of the previous segment and the tragedy of the death.

Some relation does exist between the two segments, as the child's death might evoke the memory of isolation in Linz. Nonetheless, the Woman's isolation does not resolve her trauma from the loss of her innocence. This is punctuated by the structural choices of the text. Zweig devotes a portion of the text to the child's death, which delays the woman's move to Innsbruck in the novella. Simultaneously, the section concerning the child's death prevents the trauma depicted in the previous section to evolve into isolation. In this manner, death acts as a textual border, buffering between subjects and preventing the natural progression of events in chronological order, displacing them both in time and theme.

In this manner, death is always affecting the reading, reminding readers that they are not seeing a development of a story but rather a recollection of events from the perspective of death. This even occurs in the midst of the presentation of events. Often in the text, events presented in the past are positioned in the woman's present by shifting her perspective from the time of writing the letter to past events.

Such is the case when the woman describes her emotions while going up to R.'s apartment with him for the first time. She is described in a turmoil of emotions at that point in the past, giving the occasion a feeling of intensity and immediacy. However, this sensation is quickly curtailed as the woman comments that "Even now I can hardly think of it without tears, and I have none left" (443). The phrase "hardly now" displaces the narration from the present while the woman's lack of tears alludes to the death of her child. This sentence denies the tension generated in the narrative by the event portrayed. By displacing the event in time, the notion that the event is unfolding and that something is about to happen to the woman in the story is nullified. Readers become aware that the story is a recollection and that the conclusion of events has already been revealed: the woman has failed to create a relationship with R. Furthermore, the reference to the child's death forces a comparison between it and the scene presented. The ultimate tragedy of the novella trivializes the sexual encounter which further deflates the scenes dramatic tension. Death prevents the story from becoming a consecutive accumulation of events intrinsically connected. The events described do not reverberate with one another, as in the film, but only with the woman's perspective from her point in the future. The story is a collection of disrupted events, each an isolated spot in time, looked back at in the moment of death. This mournful conception of time defines events as random and meaningless in the face of death. This perception of time negates any conception of a greater purpose in actions or the idyllic destiny of individuals. Much like Benjamin's analysis of the angel of history, time is an accumulation of ruins generated by life that can be seen from the external perspective (the woman's deathbed), but not redeemed into a constructed valuable whole (Benjamin 257-58).

The difference between the film and the novella lies in their conception of time. The film presents time as living events. Each moment is presented to have relation to other moments, being affected and illuminated by the past. Because of this, every moment presented matters, and actions represented can affect life, creating meaning and thematically resolving issues. In this paradigm, the individual has an active role, shaping moments and imbuing them with value through the individual's actions. Because of this, the individual is capable of change. They can learn and grow to improve themselves and redeem their existence. As such, the story presented in the film is a cohesive whole, its scenes sharing tight connections with one another that permeate the redemption of the characters and produce both Liza and Brand's individual growth. Ultimately, the film is hopeful, attributing a vitality to human life that allows for creation of meaning through actions.

This difference between the hopeful ideology of the film and the ultimately pessimistic viewpoint of the novella is epitomized by their respective conclusions. In the film, we see Brand's image washed over with images from Liza's history as we have seen it in the film. He then goes on to fulfill the framing story of the film, to take part in a duel that concludes his latest affair. The duel will be the end of Brand's life (Mulvey 19). The film gives us an effective image of Liza and a glorified image of Brand. Their relationship is not wasted but rather comes to fruition through their idyllic representation in the film. Conversely, the novella uses the ending to question the concept of individuality completely. The woman's very existence is destabilized as she is represented as a product of art and finally fades into the background of life. Through this move, the novella conveys the loss of human vitality in modern life and the dark future in store for modern society, while the ending of the film represents a positive, romantic ending through its final representation of the two major characters. Both Liza and Brand ascend their respective obstacles in this scene and become positive, individual and meaningful figures. This is done by the complete individualization of Liza in Brand's eyes, which changes him and prompts him to complete the task he set out to do.

In the final scene, Liza is completely perceived by Brand, leading to her utter individualization. The images washing over Brand in this scene symbolize the aggregation of all the memories recounted in the film into a single entity. Brand perceives the recollections and unites them into a single image, the passage of Liza's life which he has finally become aware of. Furthermore, the action of Brand's butler in naming the woman defines this united image. Names act as references, allowing for the identification of an entity with everything that is intrinsic to their existence. By giving Liza a name she becomes an object that can be understood and identified by Brand and so an individual, a single figure that includes unique memories and emotions.

As a complete figure, Liza is able to affect Brand and even redeem him (Wilson). Brand is redeemed morally in the film as he decides to proceed with the duel incurred by his irresponsible and destructive behavior. The duel symbolizes the punishment for Brand's behavior as a Don Juan-like character. By choosing to face his punishment, Brand takes responsibility for how he affects others. In this manner Liza redeems Brand's flawed character, providing him with moral ascension. Moreover, in his article on the film, Hunt describes Brand as an interrupted character, incapable of completing any task he sets out to do. Hunt gives several examples of this in the film, including his failed music career. The processes of his many affairs also act as a form of interrupted relationship, taken up by Brand and then unceremoniously abandoned. Hunt even goes to claim that the entire events of the film, the reading of Liza's letter, come as an interruption to Brand's preparation for the duel. However, by the end of the film he has completed two tasks—reading Liza's letter and going to the duel. This fact shows that the letter has successfully altered Brand, turning him into an individual capable of performing a complete action. He has inspected his moral inventory and has come to terms with his own past, uniting his identity with his history and conceiving of himself, as he does with Liza after reading the letter, as a conscious, self-aware character. As a result, by having an effect on Brand, Liza accomplishes her purpose in life. In the film, Liza sets out to have an effect on Brand's life. By being individualized, she causes an alteration in

Brand's character and as a result affects her will on reality. Brand is recreated according to Liza's wishes as a character that perceives her and values her existence. Liza elevates Brand to being her equal and is thus united with him thematically. Thus Liza and Brand are ultimately hopeful characters, assuring individual value and representing the ability of an individual to affect the world and alter reality to fit their wishes, as well as the redemption of that individual and their actions.

The novella presents a drastically different view of the ending, with the complete destruction of the individual and its dispersal into modern culture. It does this by first rejecting the assimilation of the woman's memories into a single comprehensible image and then by transfiguring the woman into an uncertain and un-asserting symbol. The novella prevents expressed identification of the woman by her beloved. This is seen by his inability to properly recall the events described by the woman from his own memory: "Some kind of confused memory emerged of the neighbour's child, of a young girl, of a woman in a café at night, but a vague and uncertain memory [...]" (461). R. is unable to recall a single memory that he can absolutely associate with the woman. The listing of the three women shows his inability to connect all the recurrences of the woman into a single image. As a result, despite the narratives, the woman remains fragmented and is denied unification and thus individualization.

Moreover, the novella questions the woman's very existence. This is done through the use of the symbol of dreams and its effect on the epistolary genre of the novella. The memories R. attempts to recollect are compared in a simile to dreams. This simile becomes corporeal as it ends with the assertion of the sensation that those memories "were only dreams" (461). By ending the simile in this manner, its sensation is conveyed as ambiguous, and allows for two possibilities. The first is that R. feels as if his memories are dreams. In this interpretation he maintains the possibility of the memories being real, permitting the possibility that the woman is real. The second possible interpretation assumes R. believes those memories were actually dreams. This defines the woman as a fictional character and deconstructs the woman as a living person in the story of the novella. By allowing this ambiguousness, the novella destabilizes the existence of the woman.

This representation of the woman affects the genre of the novella. As an epistolary novella, the subject of writing is already foregrounded. By questioning the existence of the woman, the notion of fiction in writing is invoked. The existence of the narrative as a letter in the novella allows for further ambiguity, as no assurance is given that the woman is in fact real in the story. In this manner, the novella disrupts the woman's existence and denies her any possibility of individuality by defining her both as an accumulation of emotions and a possible piece of fiction.

The woman's lack of factual cohesiveness and ambiguous existence reconstructs the woman at the end of the novella into a figure of art. This is achieved through the poetic descriptions of the woman in the final scene. After failing to properly recall the woman, R. equates his memories of her image to "a stone shimmering and shapeless on the bed of a stream of flowing water" (461). The simile conveys the inaccessibility of the memories, but more importantly, it symbolizes the transition of R.'s thoughts from actual recollection to a symbolic mode of thought that interprets reality. By turning to this type of apprehension, the woman is no longer approached pragmatically or realistically, but rather artistically and so impersonally. This presents the woman as a symbolic accumulation of thoughts and emotions. She becomes an artistic symbol of the tragic woman instead of a unique singular person.

This representation of the woman reaches its peak with the final sentence of the novella, in which R. thinks of the woman's influence as "distant music" (461). The comparison to music is particularly enlightening, as it suggests a figure that has no form or defining corporeal properties. Music is uniquely ephemeral as a type of art, and its use in the novella conveys the ghost-like nature the woman ultimately is given. Her existence is detached from reality, haunting it and having only an ambiguous, symbolic and impersonal effect on it.

In this manner, the woman's personal tragedy becomes art, a symbol of suffering and loss, and meshes with the general ruins of human culture which inform R.'s existence. The connection between the woman's tragedy and her devolvement into culture shows the basis on which human society is constructed. The novella presents culture as being built on the ruins of past lives. This is represented by the woman's tragedy becoming art in R.'s hands. It asserts that human society operates by turning personal tragedies into art, while eliminating the individual in the process.

The salvation of Liza and Brand and its contrast to the dissipation of the woman is the crux of the cultural translation discussed here. The novella posits an individual who is lost in the constant back noise of reality, taking place in history and art as something that can be perceived but lacks any agency or identification. This modernist modal was born out of rapid and often tragic changes which took place around the turn of the century and which destabilized earlier ideals of individuality. However, this dismantled identity as it appears in the novel should not be read as deterring. By deconstructing the woman's individuality, Zweig is able to eloquently portray the intricacies of human consciousness as it overcomes time and personal interest in the novella. It is perhaps to these concepts of human greatness to which the film translation is attracted. The film attempts to introduce the impressive power of humanity depicted in the novella into its individual centric paradigm, imbuing it into Liza. What Zweig reserves for humanity as an abstract and a multitude, the film incorporates into a person. The film espouses the American fantasy of exceptionalism, which might be more inviting than the novella's view of the same story. Nevertheless, the sober, if somewhat somber, perspective of the novel could be a more discerning way to approach reality and its limitations.

From the inspection of the various elements in both texts, I have shown that the film is consistently more positive and affirming then the novella. It supports the idea of an individual and promotes the single person's significance and effect. Liza is established early in the film as an individual through her opposition to culture and her actions are promoted as being meaningful and affecting through the cohesive narrative the film composes in its use of reverberation. This is compared to the self-effacing Liza who through her language and actions denies herself volition, development and even humanity. The cohesive of the film replaces a fragmented sense of time in the original novella which denies a comforting narrative of progression, leaving events chaotic and purposeless in the stream of time.

The extreme difference found in the between two texts conveys the great cultural difference Between the European traumatized tendencies of 1922 and the developing American sensibilities of 1948. The novella's bleak view symbolizes the modernist ideas of the desolation of modern life. Zweig's woman represents the human position within this modernist paradigm, lost between ruins of culture and history. The only manner in which one can become part of this culture is through the destruction of the self, becoming impersonal enough to fit in the encyclopedic, professional society. The novella is ultimately a modernist view of reality that assumes progression of society and culture comes at the cost of destruction. The individual disappears into the masses in order to allow the progression of society and the only way to sustain one's being is through the ghostly effect of culture, which is itself disconnected from reality.

Ophüls's film attempts to redeem the lost individual of the novella. The woman is not lost in time but rather glorified in the form of Liza. The woman's self-effacement becomes Liza's willpower in the face of opposition. This is very much in line with the American notion of the heroic, self-made individual and shows a strong belief in the importance of a person over that of the collective. Thus differences between the novella and film are cultural, reflecting the attempt of American culture to redeem the lost individual of Austrian modernist culture. In promoting the meaning of the individual and its ability to affect the world and alter reality through its actions, the American film is a romantic re-imagining of the Austrian modernist novella.

WORKS CITED

Benjamin, Walter. "Thesis on the Philosophy of History." *Illuminations*. Ed. Hannah Arendt. Trans. Harry Zohn. New York: Shocken Books, 1969. 253-64.

Hunt, Lester H. "The Paradox of the Unknown Lover: A Reading of *Letter from an Unknown Woman*." *The Journal of Aesthetics and Art Criticism* 64.1 (2006): 55-66.

Letter From an Unknown Woman. Dir. Max Ophüls. Universal: 1948. DVD.

Mulvey, Laura. "Love, History and Max Ophuls: Repetition and Difference in Three Films of Doomed Romance." *Film & History: An Interdisciplinary Journal of Film and Television Studies* 43.1 (2013): 7-23.

Wilson, George. "Max Ophuls' *Letter from an Unknown Woman*." *MLN, Comparative Literature* 98.5 (1983): 1121-1142.

Zweig, Stefan. "Letter from an Unknown Woman." *The Collected Stories of Stefan Zweig*. Trans. Anthea Bell. London: Pushkin P, 2013.

McCarthyism's Discontents: Abraham Lincoln Polonsky's *The World Above*

Joshua Parker

Before and after the Second World War, Austrians and Americans alike were engaged in philosophical and political debates on both Freudianism and Communism. Across the 1930s, 1940s and 1950s, these debates sometimes overlapped or curiously intermingled. While Freud's theories had fascinated both conservative and progressive academics in the United States at the turn of the century, by the 1930s, Marxist authors and thinkers on both sides of the Atlantic had already taken quick measure of how Freud's theory of the unconscious and psychoanalysis might speak to political theory and contemporary politics. American Communism's struggles to situate itself in relation to Freudianism and psychoanalysis were ongoing throughout the 1930s and 40s, but became more pointed and personal in the early postwar years, as many American communists and fellow-travelers began to distance themselves from Stalinism.

While Freud's theories had passed into general and popular acceptance in the United States, by the late 1940s an intrinsically American worry was developing in regard to Freudian analysis's practical methods. Useful as they had proven to individuals undergoing analysis, psychoanalysis itself was increasingly observed to be essentially limited in what benefits it might offer society in general. Its central economic precept that time (for the analysand) equaled money (for the analyst) fit mainstream postwar American economic ideals, and was indeed one reason communist theorists (and states) themselves had often rejected it as inherently bourgeois. But in a postwar American society increasingly dependent on projecting its ability to offer a fast track to middle-class abundance through Fordist mass production, psychoanalysis, and public funding for psychoanalytic research, remained problematic, not because it might be theorized as elitist or inherently bourgeois, but because its results for individual analysands, each working by the timed hour with a single analyst, could not be mass-produced.

For the patriotic, patriarchal (and increasingly publicly sex-phobic) postwar United States, ready to embrace Freudianism's modernism, but bent on stridently projecting images of a healthy, prosperous, family-centered society, Freud's insistence on civilization's mutilation of the individual's erotic life, and his work on the Oedipus complex and the id, remained problematic. And while, as Kate Millet argues, for Americans from the 1930s to the 1960s, Freud may have been "the strongest individual counterrevolutionary force in the ideology of sexual politics" (178), more practically, as a means of creating a healthier society, psychoanalysis was increasingly seen as intrinsically economically unviable on an organized national scale. This chapter digs through the nuances of this development by focusing on the relationship of Freudian and Marxist theory suggested in the literary work of American author and filmmaker Abraham Lincoln Polonsky (1910-1999), whose fictions imagined the two fields of thought as they reflected society on both sides of the Atlantic. A filmmaker by trade, as Polonsky's cinematic audience was closed to him under McCarthyism, he turned to novel writing, and his *The World Above* (1951) highlights polarized sides of this contemporary debate as he sought to represent it to fellow-travelers, and to a wider American readership.

Today best-known as a pioneer of film noir, Polonsky was born in the Bronx in 1910 to Russian Jewish immigrants. After receiving a law degree from Columbia University in 1935, he began editing a popular left-wing newspaper, *The Home Front*, before his interest in filmmaking led him to sign a screenwriter's contract with Paramount Pictures. In 1943, Polonsky put his Paramount contract on hold to serve with the U.S. Office of Strategic Services in Europe. This was work he was encouraged to continue until 1945, not despite his leftist leanings, but because of them. The Strategic Services (a federal intelligence agency that preceded the CIA) considered American-born leftists the most reliably anti-fascist agents during wartime. After the war, Polonsky published fiction in *The American Mercury* during the journal's last years as a fairly progressive publication, before its conservative turn as *The New American Mercury* after 1950, while continuing to write for Paramount. He wrote the screenplay for Robert Rossen´s independently-produced *Body and Soul* (1947), which was nominated for an Academy Award, then directed *Force of Evil* (1948). Meanwhile, Polonsky was editing the *Hollywood Quarterly*, a left-wing journal. In 1951, the journal changed hands, and Polonsky's career as a director was put on pause when he refused to testify before the U.S. House of Representatives' Un-American Activities Committee (HUAC).

At House hearings, Polonsky was called a "very dangerous citizen." In a 1999 interview, he recalled having been written up by at least one Los Angeles newspaper editor as "the most dangerous man in America" (Davis).

In any case, he was blacklisted for eighteen years. Like many Americans getting news of Stalin's atrocities in the 1950s, Polonsky cancelled his membership in the American Communist Party but, both privately and at times very publicly, remained faithful to his own thoughts on Marxist political theory, telling the *Los Angeles Times* even as late as the 1990s that "I thought Marxism offered the best analysis of history, and I still believe that" (Project Gutenberg Self-Publishing Press). Polonsky publicly objected when director Irwin Winkler rewrote his script for *Guilty by Suspicion* (1991), a film about the Hollywood blacklist era, by casting a lead character reminiscent of director Elia Kazan (Robert De Niro) as a liberal, rather than as a Communist (Bigsby). Until his death, Polonsky was a virulent critic of Kazan, who had testified before the HUAC and provided names to the Committee.

Perhaps fearing his fate in advance, Polonsky had already turned to writing fiction with *The World Above*, and would turn to literature again with *A Season Of Fear* (1956), a novel more explicitly addressing McCarthyism's effects on society and individuals caught in its web. While blacklisted, Polonsky continued writing film scripts under various pseudonyms that have never been revealed, and eventually taught philosophy at the University of Southern California's School of Cinema-Television. His next openly-directed film *Tell Them Willie Boy Is Here* (1969), starring Robert Redford, was followed by *Avalanche Express* (1979) and *Monsignor* (1982). As he published novels, essays and interviews throughout the 1970s, 1980s and 1990s, his own blacklisting (and that of his peers) was a recurrent theme touched on with continued defiance and without remorse. In 1997, the West branch of the Writers Guild of America gave him credit as the screenwriter of *Odds Against Tomorrow* (1959). Polonsky died in Beverly Hills, at 88, and received the Career Achievement Award of the Los Angeles Film Critics Association that same year, in 1999. Yet it was his blacklisting and exclusion from filmmaking in the 1950s and 1960s which had allowed him time to explore psychoanalysis and Freudian theory through literature. His work led him to take Vienna as a setting for his fiction, the city where Freud himself had lived and worked until his own, more dramatic, "blacklisting" and flight from Austria in 1938.

Much as Polonksy himself was "in many ways an odd target for the blacklist" (Oliver), the work of this aging Beverly Hills filmmaker is probably the last places one would expect to find an impassioned debate about the possibility of Freudian analysis's usefulness to a Communist society or postwar America. But this is just the issue his almost 500-page *The World*

Above took up, published the year Polonsky refused to testify at the HUAC. His biographer Alan M. Wald has called *The World Above* Polonsky's "one masterpiece," a novel "perfectly at home in the 1930s tradition of social realism" (225). It is, Wald writes, "a complex challenge not only to a world order ruled by capitalism but to orthodox Marxism itself" (225). Like William Gibson's *The Cobweb* (1954), it is a Marxist novel by a former Communist addressing psychology and psychoanalysis. Polonsky's "radical" socialist-realist novel grapples partially with social and political issues of the 1930s, 40s and 50s, but also much more deeply with how to apply Austrian psychiatric philosophy and theory in a very practical American way. If it foresees the troubles Freudian analysis would later confront in the face of the increasing popularity of psychotherapeutic drugs, its outlook is in retrospect more hopeful, for Freudianism and for humanity, than might be expected.

Polonsky's fictional protagonist Carl Meyer is a German-American, rising, in the land of opportunity, from a working-class background to laboratory work in 1930s New York, performing experimental neurosurgery on rats. When his laboratory's funding is cut, Carl takes a position in Vienna, where he turns from exploring physical neurobiology to more purely psychological and psychoanalytic research on the human mind. It is, for the young American doctor, a fascinating time to be working in Austria, but frightened by the society he witnesses, and finally finding himself "left adrift in Vienna during the rise of fascism," Carl completes his research and returns to the United States, "pledged to search for a new method of psychoanalysis" (Wald 226). This brings out a conflict in Carl's philosophical approach to human consciousness between the purely biological (represented by Polonsky through the contemporary United States) and the psychic (which Polonsky represents through the image of Austria and more generally, of Europe). For a novel aimed at a popular American audience, this is a binary pair whose commonalities and oppositions are not always entirely obvious. The "pro-Pavlov" and "anti-Freudian" campaigns that had infused debates among Communist or Socialist-leaning American psychiatric circles were largely imported from the Soviet Union and, as Wald writes, "European parties" (229).

Carl's encounter with interwar Vienna begins with a postcard invitation from an American colleague there, laden with typical stereotypes in its promises of "thorough science," "fine food," "women cheap and plentiful because they are starving" and "fairy night clubs and the sex-ridden Freudians." Carl is disgusted by the exploitative tone of his wealthy American colleague's postcard: "come to Vienna and study man's nervous system while you titillate your own." But he longs to join him in Vienna, where "the real work" is being done, as he imagines, among "the quiet labs, the libraries, the pleasures of learning" all "somehow peaceful and deep, as if life were a well-stocked ocean liner adrift eternally on a southern sea" (19).

Outside the lab, Carl's experience in Vienna is summed up in a "summer night in a Viennese café" (79). As he and a colleague discuss the over-simplicity of behavioralist, Pavlovian logic and Freudianism's fascinating depths and nuances, their conversation is interrupted by "three young Nazis" catching "an old Jew" to pull him along by his beard. Anti-Semitism is described as "ringing" society's Pavlovian bell, as Austrians, expecting "the gates of Paradise to open," with the official arrival of Nazism in 1938, instead find, "low and behold, it is Hell" (79). Carl's colleague, urging him to return to the United States, also urges him to continue exploring Freudianism rather than attach himself to simplistic schools of American behavioralism.

Back in the United States, Carl finds his training in Vienna has left him with "an easy, flexible presence which did not assert itself, but seemed to rest balanced against any turn of events, a mark of extreme egotism or capability" (84). Yet, for all his newly-acquired European polish, Carl is quickly branded by the American scientific community as "[a] God-damned Freudian," "a witch doctor who believes in psychic reality, a medievalist" who imagines "immaterial things can cause actions," while real scientists, his colleagues complain, "have been burned on crosses to disprove it" (93). Vienna, even as the center of cutting-edge psychoanalytic theory, is linked to the past—here, even to the Middle Ages—and later Carl's closest colleague and his wife will soon "gaily recall their courtship and life in old Vienna," their memories "like old waltz tunes." Carl's colleague and mentor suggests that "You can tell you're really old when you hang on to life just to remember the past and not to imagine the future," yet insists Carl himself, with his new Old World training, is "the future" (205).

As Carl's mentor dies and the Second World War begins, he finds himself physically cut off from Europe. New York City assaults Carl "like chemical shock" (274), the same method his American nemesis employs on patients. Carl finds himself staring out at a darkened New York harbor. "Behind the ocean where the war was," Polonsky's narrator intones,

> the cities no longer contended with the blackness of night but welcomed it as their future, and their ancient towers, willful as the

> unconscious, had been in darkness for centuries anyway, unserved, immobile as rock crystals, milestones in time. This road of hours along which history marched its horrors stretched out even more distantly than the theories which peopled it with progress, and each civilization as it withered on the way left there the towers which it had ambitiously raised. (273)

New York's great skyscrapers, "if not economical," Polonsky suggests, are like the great towers of pre-modern Europe: "always necessary for they asserted the existence of power, of the expanding energy which had lifted them, of the church triumphant, of the Saracen war lords, of the spendthrift Renaissance; and when those monuments still were served by men then the civilization was pressing on to its destiny, and when they lay back in time no longer served then destiny had overtaken them and the power was gone and dead." As "the skyline of the Empire City, New York, came into view through the clear cold darkness, its great towers glittering with light, hard and faceted like those of the instinctual insect, dominating the entrance to home," Carl decides that "only here, and not in Europe where the armies were, was the real energy of his time, and that here the pious service was made before the towers, and here these towers marked that concentration of energy, skill and ambition with which men everywhere would have to reckon if not love" (273). American idealism may not be ideal, Polonsky suggests, but, geopolitically, America is where the most important work is to be done.

Polonsky's novel heavily underlines two conflicting approaches to psychology by juxtapositioning two rival scientists, Carl Meyer himself and his alter ego, Val Curtin, who is "more rigidly bound to formal, biologically based scientific procedures" (Wald 226). Early in *The World Above*, the two men argue over the merits of treatment either by "talk therapy" or insulin shock—and, between the two of them, end up killing their shared patient. Carl's return to America from his studies in Vienna signals an "historical approach to the problem of mental illness" (Wald 227), reflecting Polonsky's own neo-Freudian beliefs that "the world above" (consciousness) is inevitably guided by "the world below" (Freud's unconscious). Much as Polonsky himself probed "how one lives one's life beyond ideology" (Wald 229), Carl will, in the end, become certain that mental illness is a signal of social illness.

Still marked by his research in Vienna, Carl continues his practition of Freudian theory, though his study is now criticized not only theoretically, but politically and socially: "what's the use of the whole thing, what's the use of finding a way to help a thousand men, or ten thousand, when in one year ten million of them are ground up into hamburger and mud, on battlefields and in cities, men, women, children, good, bad, indifferent? What's the use of it?" (296). In America, the postwar "Neo-Pavlovianism" of B.F. Skinner's behavioralism has "a tendency to become mechanical and faddist, running after drugs, shocks, disciplines and other gross alterations based on the notion that it was the nervous system itself that had to be readjusted. Its practitioners would not be at all surprised to find a vaccine or serum that could do the trick" of solving mental illness or even society's more general ills. On the other hand, Carl worries, the "historical school," as Polonsky calls European theory, "while it had discovered various psychic mechanisms that applied in all cases, at the end and most logically got to the point in which every case was special, every treatment personal, and every perfect cure interminable. [...] Only a general theory of causation could save this science from becoming a rather subtle form of artistic expression" (301-02). While American-style materiality and mass production, Polonsky underlines, is blunt and has limits in its usefulness, the theoretical craftsmanship of European individualism, or elitism, likewise cannot offer societal solutions in itself. The technique of the former must be applied to the latter. Freudianism must become an applied science.

As the head of a new American mental hospital Carl joins insists, taking up Carl's own theories: "We don't try to send back one of those useless finished psychological products, a less troublesome *sick* man. We send back a troubled, seeking creature, a man who wants something from life, who will struggle to achieve it, not at the expense of his own personality, but in struggle with the society which has created him and maimed him" (311). As society itself is the cause of its own ills, those suffering from them must be "cured" only in order to work to "cure" the society which has caused their illness. This Marxist psychiatry is a way of healing society through the individual patient. In this view, psychiatrists are "a group of men and women devoted to truth, and as such, blessed, fortunate to have near us these strange, sensitive creatures of our age, people called the mentally ill, but who are in reality the socially ill" (312). Polonsky's struggle with the individualism of Freudianism, its non-adaptability to that typically American tendency toward mass use and production, finally underlines the curious resonances between Communism and American-style Fordism, hinting some form of Communism itself is essentially in step with contemporary American ideals.

Polonsky suggested it was much more in step with America's ideals than were the growing privatization and corporatization of the Great Depression's close, as the United States was on its way to becoming the strongest force in the postwar world sphere.

Polonksy's novel has Carl called to testify in a congressional hearing over a potential withdrawal of his research funding, a trial Polonsky modeled on the 1946 HUAC hearings in which the Hollywood Ten were investigated. Much in the vein of social realism, other political issues in Polonsky's novel are personified by characters. Carl's friend David, for example, Wald suggests, "personifies the spirit of the New Deal," as it is "transformed into a burgeoning imperial authority that seeks to replace the old colonial powers as the global guardian of an expanding capitalist system" (227). Carl's love object and sometime lover is clearly aligned with the working class. His senators are bald representatives of beltway insiders with their ears bent to lobbyists.

The World Above closes by insisting Marxism's essential vision is an essentially American one, despite its condemnation by the Washington court to which Carl is convened to either defend or lay aside his theories. "Only when man was looked at not as mind reflecting or inventing the universe, but as an animal in conflict with it, an animal whose consciousness was part of his struggle with society and nature, part of his relation to it, part of his gift to it," Carl believes, "only when the mind was not removed from existence but discovered to be its creature, only then was a rational science of psychology actually possible" (353). The federally-funded American hospital Carl runs works with posttraumatic stress disorders caused by the Second World War, and Carl assumes that in the postwar landscape of America, "the war today is the peace around us" (353). Social and political conservatism have created invalids, leaving paranoia and mental illness in their wake. The novel allowed Polansky to reveal what he believed to be Freud's usefulness to Marxianism, and Marx's usefulness to political theory, to sociology, and to society more generally: "no science of psychology can be founded on what man is, but only on what man is becoming, the general rule being that he is never becoming anything but what society itself is becoming" (354). It was a pointed outlook, in a time when men were being called by their government to make public statements (or decisions) on their beliefs. The final criticism of postwar America in Polonsky's novel is that it has given itself over to the development of "the World Above." This means it has given itself over to the glittering urban towers and the power of the wealthy as opposed to that of "the world below" of the working class, and, more pointedly, to "the world above" of surface consciousness and materialism, as opposed to examining its own national collective unconscious more deeply in order to cure itself.

After pleading the Fifth Amendment before the HUAC in 1951, Polansky himself espoused Marxism while rejecting Stalinism throughout his life, holding lucidly to his political thoughts even into his 80s. His protagonist Carl asks toward the novel's end, "How can we influence [people in the field] if we deny the validity [to the committee] of what we're trying to preach?" (447). As Polonsky told an interviewer at the *Los Angeles Times* in 1968, when interviewed about his own refusal to testify before the HUAC, "If you said you were sorry you were a radical and had seen the errors of your ways, you were let off. That's like saying you have no right to make political experiments in your mind. That's the kind of thing they do in Communist countries, but we're supposed to be a free country. We need to be a genuinely free country and not merely pretend to be one" (Oliver). During the years of his blacklisting, Polonsky was able to work less directly but no less profoundly, speaking to a much-reduced audience, through literature, his plots and settings stretching the Atlantic to an Austria whose recent politics and political climate, he felt, held, like the depths of the unconscious itself, insights into America's own postwar psychic ills.

Like Polansky himself, Carl refuses to recant his ideas, even if this might have allowed him to continue his work while quietly following them, and even though his hospital's director does. "A leap in history had separated" the two opposing men in Polonsky's novel (470), one willing to recant his beliefs in order to follow his dreams, and the other unwilling to recant them even if it meant being unable to. Under McCarthyism, the novel suggests, the United States' originary ideals, like those of "old Europe," had become history.

Works Cited

"Abraham Polonsky." *Project Gutenberg Self-Publishing P*. Web. 11 Oct. 2015.

Bigsby, Christopher. *Arthur Miller*. Cambridge, MA: Harvard UP, 2011.

Davis, Charles. Interview with Abraham Polonsky. 6 July 1999. Web. 11 Oct. 2015.

Millet, Kate. *Sexual Politics*. Garden City, New York: Doubleday & Company, 1970.

Oliver, Myrna. "Hollywood Blacklist's Abraham Polonsky Dies." *Los Angeles Times*, 28 Oct. 1999. Web. 11 Oct. 2015.

Polonsky, Abraham. *The World Above*. 1951. Chicago: U of Illinois P, 1999.

Wald, Alan M. *American Night: The Literary Left in the Era of the Cold War*. Chapel Hill: U of North Carolina P, 2012.

The Austrian State Treaty and American Foreign Policy

Dante Mazzari

Introduction

In February 1955, Vyachislav Molotov, the Soviet Foreign Minister, in a speech to the Supreme Soviet announced that the Soviet Union would be willing to consider the question of an Austrian treaty separately from the German question. This represented a major reversal of policy for the Soviet Union, which since 1945 had insisted that in order to prevent a second *Anschluss*, an Austrian settlement could only be reached after a final peace treaty with Germany, an eventuality which would only come to pass after German reunification in 1990. The statement was followed rapidly by consultation with the Austrian government, culminating in a visit to Moscow by Chancellor Julius Raab in April and discussions with the Western Allies resulting in the signing of a State Treaty, the only one of its kind, in May 1955. The following November, the last allied troops left Austria and parliament declared Austria's permanent neutrality.

By the standards of the early Cold War, the rapidity of these developments was astonishing. As 1955 dawned, after a decade without any progress on the issue, Austria was the last county in Europe legally under allied occupation. Austria, moreover, would represent the only place in Europe where Soviet troops withdrew from positions held during the Second World War and the only European country in which neutrality was guaranteed by the four allied powers (in this way the Austrian case was different from that of Finland). The State Treaty furthermore represented the first agreement between the Soviets and the Western Allies since the 1949 Berlin Blockade: a rare accord amidst a series of confrontational actions and deteriorating East-West relations. 1955 can be said to be the year in which Cold War lines were frozen after a decade of fluidity, as West Germany joined NATO and the Warsaw Pact was concluded. In the midst of this, the Austrian State Treaty was a unique case which had an amplified regional and international effect, aiding Soviet overtures to neutral countries such as Yugoslavia and Egypt and exerting a pull on the small countries of the newly created

Warsaw Pact. American officials, meanwhile, largely viewed the treaty as an extension of the German question and in many ways failed to appreciate its significance in the context of Central Europe.

While the Austrian State Treaty has been the subject of considerable study in Austrian sources, there is relatively little scholarship on this issue in English. Except for a few significant studies published within ten years of the Treaty's ratification, there has been little recent work setting the Treaty in an international context and American primary sources, significantly those published as part of the *Foreign Relations of the United States* series, on which in large part this essay relies, remain understudied.

HISTORICAL BACKGROUND 1943-55

The 1943 Moscow Declaration by the United States, the United Kingdom, and the Soviet Union declared the *Anschluss* "null and void" and characterized Austria as "the first free country to fall victim to Hitlerite aggression." Beyond that there was little agreement among the allies on what postwar Austria should look like. When Soviet troops liberated Austria in April 1945, they unilaterally set up a provisional government, initially led by the Social Democrat leader Karl Renner with Communists in several key posts, most notably the Interior Ministry. This action, which followed a pattern strikingly similar to that taken in other countries the Red Army liberated, did much to persuade the Western allies of the necessity of setting up a divided occupation regime the following July. Renner, however, moved quickly to hold elections and was able to secure a firm democratic mandate for his provisional government, ensuring its authority was extended into all four occupied zones. The elections resulted in a left-right coalition between the Social Democrats and the People's Party and amounted to a crushing defeat for the Communists, who won barely five percent of the vote.

The Communist party's failure to gain traction in Austria, and its later failure to make gains out of labor unrest in 1950, meant that the Soviet Union had little reason to hope Austria could be incorporated into the Eastern Bloc and little direct interest in negotiating an Austrian settlement. The continued occupation, moreover, ensured the steady flow of valuable Austrian war reparations. In 1946 the Red Army seized two major Austrian banks, the Creditanstalt and the Länderbank, for example, and established control over shipping on the Danube. Most importantly for Soviet strategic objectives, they also seized the Zistersdorf oil fields and began shipping critically needed petroleum back to the Soviet Union.

The Western allies, for their part, had waived their right to reparations from Austria, and were broadly friendly to the Austrian provisional government, though they remained concerned that negotiation on the Austrian question could disrupt a united front on European security issues. As will be discussed, American policymakers saw Austria essentially as an extension of the German question and therefore, while they were broadly sympathetic to the Austrian case, in the face of Soviet resistance, they largely calculated that any potential gains that might result from negotiations on Austria were outweighed by the risks of allowing the Soviets to disrupt Western unity.

That left the initial proposal for neutrality to the Austrian political leadership. Neutrality had entered the Austrian political lexicon in 1947 when Renner had endorsed it publicly, following which the Social Democrats included it in their electoral platform. In 1953, a backchannel overture was made to the Soviets through the good offices of India, as a result of a meeting between Foreign Minister Karl Gruber and Jawaharlal Nehru in Bürgenstock, Switzerland (Ionescu). This met with some approval from Moscow and at the Berlin conference in 1954, the Soviets made neutrality a condition of an Austrian treaty. This provision, however, was for the moment seen as incidental as official Soviet policy still considered any Austrian settlement contingent on the frozen issue of the German peace treaty.

Soviet Motivations

By January 1955 the proposal of neutrality had begun to look more appealing from the Soviet perspective. The conditions of continued Soviet presence on Austrian soil had by that time shifted substantially. Soviet domestic oil production had tripled in the ten years after the Second World War, thereby negating the need for Austria's most valued form of reparation. With the Soviet normalization of relations with East Germany, there was no longer any significant strategic advantage to stationing troops on Austrian soil. Moreover, Austria was the only country to host Soviet troops which had a free press and an unsympathetic government. This exposed the Soviets to both hostile Austrian public opinion and a world opinion which was largely sympathetic to the Austrian cause at a time when Moscow was anxious to portray the Soviet Union as a force for peace.

If in a general sense, Austria had become more of a liability than an asset under occupation, the precise timing of the Soviet reversal was certainly caused by the rearmament of West Germany. Between 1950 and 1953, negotiations between the Soviet Union and the Western allies on European issues were effectively frozen by the Korean War. In 1954, having been given new impetus by the war, the Western allies ratified the Paris Pact, which restored West German sovereignty and allowed for rearmament conditional on NATO membership, which became effective in 1955. This move was strongly opposed by the Soviets, though, having already established normal relations with the German Democratic Republic in East Germany, they were left with few options to counter it.

Neutrality for Germany had been proposed several times since the end of the Second World War but by 1955 had ceased to be a realistic option. The United States, as chief proponent of West German NATO membership, was unwilling to consider any proposal which might undermine rearmament. Soviet propaganda did to some extent endorse neutrality—and linked it with the possibility of reunification—but the Soviets were wary of anything that might lead to elections in East Germany which could force a Soviet withdrawal, thereby threatening the satellite system.

Austrian neutrality, on the other hand, held several compelling advantages for the Soviets. First, it ensured that Austria would not become a member of NATO, thereby insulating Hungary and the southern border of Czechoslovakia from the alliance's borders. Second, it afforded a way for the Soviets to withdraw from an unpopular occupation without giving the appearance of retreat. Third, it allowed the Soviets to change the narrative of West German rearmament. Instead of appearing as though West Germany was rearming in the face of Communist aggression in Eastern Europe, Soviet sponsorship of Austrian neutrality allowed Soviet propaganda to portray West German rearmament as Western militarism in the face of Soviet willingness to negotiate.

Austrian neutrality did however present a more roundabout challenge to the Soviet strategic position in Eastern Europe. Under the Potsdam Agreement, the legal basis for the continuing presence of Soviet troops in Hungary and Romania was as a means of protecting supply lines to its occupying army in Austria (Ferring). As the Soviet Union already had peace agreements with Hungary and Romania, signing a treaty with Austria would in theory require it to evacuate all three countries. While few observers imagined a Soviet evacuation of Hungary and Romania was imminent, signing an Austrian settlement would create a legal challenge to the continued troop presence in these satellite countries a time when the the Kremlin wanted the Soviet Union to be seen as a defender of sovereignty under international law.

This dilemma was solved though the establishment of the Warsaw Pact, which served both as a collective security agreement and allowed for the stationing of Soviet troops in member countries. So closely were these issues bundled that when Molotov arrived at the Belvedere Palace in Vienna for the signing of the Austria State Treaty, he came directly from Warsaw where he had been to ratify the pact only the day before. His trip had both guaranteed perpetual neutrality for Austria and permanently ruled it out for any of the satellite countries.

Regional and International Ramifications

Sponsoring neutrality also had another, more specific appeal to Soviet foreign policy. Before his death, in 1952 Stalin had begun to promote the "new look," which encouraged tolerance of and engagement with neutralist countries, and a refocus away from Europe towards the Third World. Throughout the 1950s, the diplomatic successes of the non-aligned movement meant that alienating major neutralist countries was losing the Soviets influence in Asia and Africa just as the unity of the world communist movement was crumbling under pressure from Yugoslavia and, eventually, China. In addition to being able to shift the blame for the rearmament of West Germany, the Austrian settlement had the effect of signaling Soviet endorsement of neutrality as a policy. This new posture helped smooth relations with major neutral countries such as India, who had played a role in securing Austrian neutrality, and Egypt which announced a strategic partnership with the Soviet Union the following year. Most importantly, Soviet sponsorship of a neutral Austria was a specific appeal to Yugoslavia, both because of its shared (and disputed) border with Austria and its prominent role in the non-aligned movement. Within a year of the Austrian State Treaty being signed, Khrushchev made his historic visit to Belgrade which began the process of Soviet-Yugoslav rapprochement.

In a 1959 post-mortem in *Foreign Affairs* Bruno Kreisky postulated that from the Soviet perspective, Austrian neutrality was intended to tempt smaller European countries away from NATO (Gruber). With the possible exception of Sweden this does not seem to have been the case. The greater pull was in the other direction: on those small countries who had newly been brought into the Warsaw Pact, especially those who had historically been part of the Austro-Hungarian Empire. Neutrality was considered so threatening to the communist government in Romania, for example, a country itself known for pursuing a divergent foreign policy, that discussing neutralism was criminalized under penalty of death in 1956 (Ionescu). The appeal of Austrian-style neutrality was especially strong in Hungary where the Hungarian revolution broke out nearly a year to the day after the evacuation of Allied troops from Austria. Imre Nagy's declaration of neutrality on November 1, 1956 and the implications Hungary's withdrawal would have had on the newly formed Warsaw Pact, was a major motivating factor behind the subsequent Soviet intervention. As the Hungarian revolution was being crushed, the Suez Crisis was coming to a head, encouraged by the Soviets' new embrace of neutralist Egypt.

AMERICAN REACTIONS

It is fair to say American policy-makers essentially failed to grasp the international ramifications of Austrian neutrality. In 1955, U.S. policy in Europe was focused squarely on ensuring the implementation of the Paris Accords, which went into effect on May 5, 1955, ten days before the Austrian State Treaty was signed. Given this overarching objective, and the certainty of Soviet opposition, it is perhaps not surprising that Austrian issues were afforded a lesser priority than West German rearmament. Given the levels of mistrust between the United States and the Soviet Union at this time, it is also perhaps not surprising that the U.S. State Department initially reacted to the Soviet offer to discuss an Austrian State Treaty with distrust. The level of distrust was such, however, that virtually no senior voices in the State Department were prepared to take the Soviet offer at face value.

What exactly the Soviets were trying to accomplish was a matter of some debate. The assumption of the most senior staff, including Secretary of State John Foster Dulles, was that either this was an attempt to tempt the West Germans into adopting neutrality by holding out the possibility of reunification (something the Soviet press had called for) or it was an attempt to disrupt unity between the Western allies before the Paris Pact could be implemented. There was also an understanding that appearing conciliatory on Austrian issues was a way of gaining a propaganda victory out of West German rearmament.

Though it was largely left unsaid, American policymakers would have recognized that the Austrian settlement represented Soviet fulfillment of one of the Western conditions for a four power summit. In July 1955, heads of state of the four allied powers met in Geneva for the first time since the Potsdam Conference in 1945. The Soviets had repeatedly called for a summit since Stalin's death in 1953 and the Eisenhower administration had consistently refused, not wanting to give the Soviets a larger stage in light of increasing international tensions. What the State Department likely did not fully understand at the time, was that in the murky aftermath of Stalin's death, calling a four power summit had become a personal priority for Nikita Khrushchev, as much to solidify his own position as to achieve any specific foreign policy objective (Khrushchev would attend the 1955 Geneva summit as head of the Communist Party of the Soviet Union, alongside Nikolai Bulganin who was actually head of state). Where later accounts from the State Department (including *FRUS*) mention the Austrian State Treaty, it is frequently in the context of the Geneva summit.

It is clear that the Soviet offer caught the Americans off guard. There were, however, compelling reasons for ending the occupation of Austria from an American perspective. The United States had already accepted Austrian neutrality in principle and there was little appetite for continuing an occupation which had, from the outset, been seen as a burden. By 1955, there was little strategic value to the presence of U.S. troops on Austrian soil and, while most of the Austrian press still blamed the Soviets for the continued occupation, the State Department was acutely aware that they were also continually in danger of running afoul of Austrian public opinion. Cables from the U.S. Embassy in Vienna from this period, included in the FRUS series, indicate a high level of concern about press criticism of the United States and about the loose talk of American soldiers in Austria.

So pervasive was the pessimism regarding relations with the Soviet Union that no senior policy makers appear to have regarded the Soviet offer as genuine. Meeting with the Austrian ambassador before Julius Raab's visit to Moscow, Dulles himself warned the Austrian not to get his hopes up, while making it clear they were anxious to sign a treaty if the conditions were right

(FRUS). The State Department was aware, moreover, that the Austrians were adamant about moving quickly to secure a treaty before the deal could fall apart and was anxious not to stand in their way.

It is clear that U.S. policymakers had every reason to support the Austrians with cautious optimism, even if they viewed the Soviet offer primarily as a ruse. How, though, did they miss the international dimension? And what effect might greater understanding of the neutrality issue have had on U.S. policy towards the region?

This was a period of American history in which foreign policy was very tightly centralized around Eisenhower and Dulles and a circle of their key senior advisors. In this case that also included two giants in the field of Soviet relations: Charles Bohlen, then Ambassador to the Soviet Union and a highly respected Soviet analyst, and Tommy Thompson as High Commissioner for Austria, who would later serve as Ambassador to the Soviet Union and play a crucial role as senior advisor to John F. Kennedy during the Cuban Missile Crisis. These were men with enormous experience in dealing with the Soviet Union. They were also men, Dulles especially, who subscribed to a theory about international communism which portrayed it as monolithic, Soviet-dominated, and universally menacing.

This may in part explain why there was so little consideration paid to Central and Eastern European affairs at this time, as distinct from relations with the Soviet Union. Compounding this issue was a lag in understanding how policy was made in the new Soviet Union following Stalin's death. This is understandable given the opacity of the complicated transition of power after Stalin's death, but it helped obscure Soviet motivations in consolidating power in Eastern Europe, and how the "new look" was shifting emphasis away from Europe itself. This complexity was embodied in the person of Vyachislav Molotov himself who, almost uniquely among Stalin's inner circle, survived the turmoil of Stalin's last years and continued to present the outward face of Soviet diplomacy until 1957, long after the terrain in the Kremlin had shifted. At the same time, Western confusion about the internal affairs of the satellite states and political diversity within the communist world would become especially acute in the years that followed, notably during the Hungarian revolution.

In failing to take the Soviet embrace of Austrian neutrality seriously, U.S. policymakers failed to understand the role that neutrality and neutralism played in Soviet foreign policy. It is fair to say that by 1955 there was no serious alternative to a neutral Austria—or at least no desirable alternative.

That said, a stronger understanding of how the Austrian State Treaty signaled a new Soviet tolerance for, if not embrace of, neutrality as a legitimate policy might have led to a great understanding of the Soviet relationship with Yugoslavia and with regional powers further abroad such as India and Egypt. Greater recognition of Soviet intolerance towards neutrality among the countries of the Warsaw Pact, by contrast, should have led to a more sophisticated understanding of the role of that organization and the centrifugal forces which would remain at play among the satellite states through 1989. In a period of the Cold War characterized by deep mistrust, such greater understanding might even have begun to ease U.S.-Soviet tensions.

WORKS CITED

Cullis, Michael. "The Austrian Treaty Settlement." *Review of International Studies* 7.3 (July 1981): 159-64.

Ferring, Robert L. "The Austrian State Treaty of 1955 and the Cold War." *The Western Political Quarterly* 21.4 (Dec. 1968): 651-67.

Foreign Relations of the United States (FRUS), 1955–1957, Austrian State Treaty; Summit and Foreign Ministers Meetings, 1955. Volume V. Eds. William Z. Slany and Charles S. Sampson, United States Government Printing Office (Washington) 1987.

Gruber, Karl. "Austria Infelix." *Foreign Affairs* 25.2 (Jan. 1947): 229-38.

Ionescu, Ghita. "The Austrian State Treaty and Neutrality in Eastern Europe." *International Journal* 23.3 (Summer 1968): 408-20.

Kreisky, Bruno. "Austria Draws the Balance." *Foreign Affairs* (19 Aug. 2015). Web. 19 Aug. 2015

Kunz, Josef L. "Austria's Permanent Neutrality." *The American Journal of International Law* 50.2 (Apr. 1956): 418-25.

Royal Institute of International Affairs (unattributed). "The Hard Road to an Austrian Treaty." *The World Today* 11.5 (May 1955): 190-202.

SALZBURG GLOBAL SEMINAR: 1947-2015

MARTY GECEK

Salzburg Global Seminar was founded in 1947 as the Salzburg Seminar in American Civilization by three young visionaries at Harvard University, as an international forum for young men and women who had recently been at war with each other, and who were seeking a better future for Europe and the world. One of these young visionaries was Clemens Heller, an Austrian exile who was a doctoral student in the history department. Heller felt that Austria, in the heart of Europe, was the ideal place for realizing his plan to bring together young intellectuals as a means of revitalizing intellectual life in Europe. He believed that former enemies could talk and learn from each other in a relaxed, neutral setting and spawn fresh thinking about ways forward. In a world still reeling from and ravaged by war, this notion that dialogue among unlikely associates was an essential investment for global recovery was a radical proposition—one so radical that it worked. In New York, Heller ran into Helene Thimig, a fellow Austrian whom he had known before the war. Thimig was the widow of the wealthy Austrian theater impresario and Hollywood producer Max Reinhardt, who had lived in Schloss Leopoldskron between the two World Wars. Heller expressed to Thimig his hopes for creating a seminar in Austria. Thimig was much taken with the idea and offered Schloss Leopoldskron in Salzburg, Austria for the first session.

Try to imagine Europe in 1946. Tensions were increasing among former allies, displaced persons were roaming everywhere, and Austrian and German cities were in ruin, divided into zones of military occupation. Churchill had just announced that an "iron curtain" had descended across Europe. With this background, Clemens Heller gratefully accepted Thimig's offer to hold a seminar at Schloss Leopoldskron. So, in the summer of 1947, along with Richard Campbell, Jr., a fellow Harvard student, and Scott Elledge, a young English instructor, these three young men began organizing a seminar focusing on European unity and cooperation. They raised $25,000, including money from the Rockefeller Foundation and from the Harvard Student Council, which donated the unspent balance from the Food Relief Fund which would feed the students. Halfway through the summer, money for groceries was running out, and it was thanks to several performances by a young mime from Paris, Marcel Marceau, that the seminar was able to continue (Ryback). For six weeks in the summer of 1947, 97 students from western and eastern Europe gathered at Schloss Leopoldskron, eager to learn more about the United States. Thus the curriculum included instruction in American Studies—history, the social sciences, literature, and fine arts. Most were university students or young teachers, but also artists, writers and journalists. The diverse group included a Czech who had been imprisoned at Buchenwald; an Austrian who had joined the Nazi party, fought in France and was a POW in Kentucky; a Dane who had been arrested by the Gestapo; and a woman who had seen her mother shot at Auschwitz. The distinguished faculty included Margaret Mead, the esteemed anthropologist; Vassily Leontief, the economist and future Nobel Prize Laureate; and F.O. Matthiessen, the literary historian, who in his welcome speech declared: "All of us come with a strong conviction of the values of American democracy, yet also with what I take to be a saving characteristic of American civilization: a sharp critical sense of both its excesses and its limitations" (Matthiessen 15).

They spent the summer in intellectual discussion about the culture, politics and economics of the United States. Participants were astounded that in the middle of a military zone of occupation, with military headquarters next door in the Meierhof, none of the Americans present hesitated to criticize the U.S. government. One day there was a hot debate comparing the United States and the Soviet Union, which resulted in a message being sent to Washington questioning the political reliability of Clemens Heller, calling him a dangerous Communist. But there was an American political officer from Vienna present, Martin Herz, who was impressed by the intellectual quality of the discussion and by the openness of the exchanges, and thus the seminar was allowed to continue. Following the seminar, Margaret Mead wrote: "Never doubt that a small group of thoughtful, committed citizens can change the world; indeed, it's the only thing that ever has" (Hallman 2015: 10). It is significant to note that when in the spring of 1947 George C. Marshall announced his plan for the economic rehabilitation of Europe, the Harvard students had already initiated their own "intellectual Marshall plan."

Clemens Heller, Richard Campbell, Jr. and Scott Elledge, 1947

Margaret Mead in the Chinese Room, 1947

Fellows of the first session, 1947

In the next years, the Salzburg Seminar expanded its program significantly, became an incorporated educational entity, and received regular sources of income from American foundations. At first, the sessions were so-called "General Sessions" on broad American themes, but after 1955 six sessions a year were held on specific aspects of American Studies. Faculty members were distinguished Americans such as the sociologist Daniel Bell, the historian Henry Steele Commager, American novelists Saul Bellow and Ralph Ellison. In 1953, the Salzburg Seminar held its first session on American Law and Legal Institutions, which became a very popular annual tradition, led by distinguished Harvard law faculty members such as Kingman Brewster and Paul Freund. These sessions continued each year into the 1980s, and were led by US Supreme Court justices such as Harry Blackmun, Warren Burger and in 1970 Sandra Day O'Connor, the first female Supreme Court justice. More recently, Ruth Bader Ginsburg, Anthony Kennedy and Stephen Breyer have led programs on American legal issues, and are hosts of the annual lecture on the rule of law in honor of American lawyer and presidential counsel Lloyd N. Cutler.

In the mid-1960s, the Salzburg Seminar expanded the themes of programs and places from which its Fellows came. Although early sessions included Fellows from eastern and central Europe, their numbers dwindled as East-West tensions grew. In 1965, the Seminar director traveled to Budapest,

Warsaw and Prague. He was met with a mixture of suspicion and interest at the various ministries. Czechs began coming regularly in 1966, the first Romanian in 1968, the first East German in 1973, and the first citizen of the USSR in 1978. These Fellows were not dissidents. They were selected by their ministry for their political reliability. They were reluctant to speak up in plenary sessions, but in informal discussions in the *Bierstube* in the basement of Schloss Leopoldskron, there were very honest discussions between Turks and Greeks, East and West Germans, and Russian and Americans.

Themes gradually became more international and global in focus, with fewer dedicated to American themes. For much of the Cold War the Salzburg Seminar was one of the few fora in the world where men and women from both sides of the Iron Curtain could gather in a neutral atmosphere to discuss matters of common concerns. Almost every session in these years reflected the new "internationalizing" of the programs. There were very few sessions related to American themes, and the proportions of Americans on the faculty declined considerably. Typical sessions titles were "Development, Communication and Social Change" taught by a Japanese, a Frenchman and two Austrians, one of them Hannes Androsch, who in 1973 brought the negotiation of an Austrian grant for the Seminar to a successful conclusion.

In the mid-1970s, the considerable turbulence in the Middle East led to the decision to provide a forum at Salzburg to bring potential enemies together at Schloss Leopoldskron. The Seminar President John Tuthill traveled to Saudi Arabia, Kuwait, Israel, Jordan and Egypt and found a welcome reception (Eliot and Eliot 15). These countries sent Fellows, and they in turn recommended the Seminar to their colleagues, who wanted to meet Americans and Europeans to discuss common interests. For example, Israelis and Palestinians could talk to their professional peers about economics, ecology or health care instead of the West Bank. By 1984, more than three hundred Fellows had come from Middle Eastern countries to Salzburg. Today these countries are represented in virtually every program organized at Schloss Leopoldskron. There was also expansion into Africa: in 1974 one Nigerian attended a session; ten years later there were forty-four Africans from eleven countries. The same was true of Asia. With the help of the U.S. Agency for International Development and the U.S. Information Agency, the Seminar welcomed Fellows from India and Japan. Today, in 2015, participants from many Asian countries, including China, are a part of every session. Their attendance is supported by entities such as the Japan Foundation, the Nippon Foundation and the Korea Foundation.

In the 1980s and 1990s, as global themes became dominant, there were voices lamenting the lack of any program related to the study of America—not least the many American Studies alumni. So in an effort to return to its American Studies roots, the Seminar created the American Studies Center (ASC) in 1994. This was made possible by a $9 million grant from the United States Information Agency. The founder and first director was Dr. Ronald Clifton. Between 1994 and 2003, thirty-two successful sessions on American Studies themes were organized—focusing on cultural studies, history, politics and literature (Hallman 2014: 12). Many of these sessions addressed contemporary global concerns in an American context. Participants were pre-selected by United States Information Service offices in western, eastern and central Europe, as well as a few from Asia. The director of the ASC chose the topics, the themes were communicated to the USIS offices around the world, and they made the selections. The first session in 1994 was called "On-Line Techniques." In those days, "online" was a new word to many, and the use of computers in education was very new. It was virtually non-existent in most of the countries which sent participants to Salzburg. It was gratifying to watch the reaction of a professor of English from Kazakhstan as she sent a message via her computer to her fellow participant from the Czech Republic. These professors went back to their universities and worked hard to convince their superiors that the use of computers in education was the future. This happened thirty years ago, and back then, few could imagine where technology would take us today.

The last American Studies Center session took place in 2003. By then, the USIA grant had ended and there was no outside funding in place to continue American Studies sessions. Yet there were many who felt strongly that American Studies programs, the institution's legacy, needed to be continued. In 2004, the Salzburg Seminar American Studies Association (SSASA) was founded to build on the positive momentum resulting from so many successful sessions in the past and to promote the American Studies component of the Seminar's program offerings. So while the ASC was never formally closed, it in essence became the SSASA. Clearly in today's complicated world, we need to grasp every opportunity for dialogue about America's role in a global context. Salzburg Global Seminar (its new name, to reflect its global focus), with its long history of bringing individuals together from all over the world to discuss timely issues, is uniquely placed to provide a forum for such discussion. Each year, the SSASA organizes one American Studies program on various themes, such as literature, foreign policy, history, and cultural studies. Most symposia welcome some fifty participants from about twenty-five countries around the world, who come to Schloss Leopoldskron to discuss and learn about the latest developments in the theme of the program. Many of the participants are academics teaching American Studies at the university level, who return to their classrooms with new information for their students.

In 2006, SSASA organized a symposium on "Redefining America: Race, Ethnicity and Immigration," led by distinguished scholars including the late Emory Elliott of the University of California, Riverside. There were discussions on how the literature, film, music, art and other forms of cultural production impacted the conflicts and tensions produced by rapid immigration and social changes. In November 2012 the theme was "Screening America: Film and Television in the 21st Century." There were forty-four participants from eighteen countries around the world present, plus faculty. Participants and faculty discussed the changes in the modern media, particularly in the film and television industries, and the ways in which film and television have influenced America's image around the world. Participants explored the institutional effect of film and television on the arts, technology and politics of the United States and ultimately their relation to the perception of America overseas. One particularly fascinating discussion focused on "Global Hollywood and American Politics in the Age of 9/11."

Since many American Studies academics come to the discipline through literature and cultural studies, there is always a demand for a program on American literature. In 2014 the theme was "Defining America: New Writing, New Voices, New Directions." A stellar faculty led the program, including one of America's leading Americanists, Paul Lauter; author and American Studies professor Christopher Bigsby of the University of East Anglia; Mary Pat Brady, who specializes in Latino and Latina literatures at Cornell University; and Asian-American author Karen Tei Yamashita. There were fifty-seven participants from twenty-six countries, including five Austrians. Participants and faculty discussed new voices in American literature, and the extent to which they reflect recent demographic movements and how they reshape social and creative interactions. Also important was a discussion about the changes in forms of writing, publishing and book-selling and the impact of these changes on literary expression and cultural liveliness in America today.

How has the Salzburg Global Seminar evolved in recent years? Programs are now designed around three cross-cutting clusters that reflect the values of the institution: human transformation, urban transformation and conflict transformation. Through this "triple-lens thinking," programs challenge established mindsets, inspire collaborative and impactful solutions and build lasting networks (Salzburg Global 3). In June 2013, Salzburg Global convened its first Salzburg Global LGBT Forum, called "LGBT and Human Rights: Challenges, Next Steps" (Hallman 2014: 20). While lesbian, gay, bisexual and transgender rights have become very visible in the global human rights agenda, at the same time many countries are passing increasingly regressive laws. As this inaugural session gathered at Schloss Leopoldskron, the U.S. Supreme Court was hearing cases for and against the Defense of Marriage Act, and France had just signed both gay adoption and gay marriage into law. Against the backdrop of growing rights as well as persistent persecution in some areas of the world, more than sixty representatives of LGBT activist and human rights organizations, legal experts, journalists, academics and philanthropists joined for a global discussion on the status of LGBT rights worldwide, and how equal rights for LGBT people around the world can be best advanced, both locally and globally. The purpose of the Salzburg Global LGBT Forum is to build a network of support and knowledge across the more than fifty countries on six continents in which it now has members, and to build new alliances and strengthen fundamental human rights for all, regardless of sexual orientation and gender identity.

Fellows meeting in the library of Schloss Leoploldskron

Another exciting initiative is the series entitled "Holocaust Education and Genocide Prevention" that began in 2010 and takes place each year. In 2012 Salzburg Global held a three-day symposium hosted by the Salzburg Global Seminar and the U.S. Holocaust Memorial Museum. Held—as most Salzburg Global programs are—at Schloss Leopoldskron, once home to the local Nazi party leader, experts from across the globe considered the value of Holocaust education in a global context. Participants came from countries as diverse as Mexico and South Korea, as well as from countries that have suffered their own ethnic violence and genocides, such as Cambodia and Armenia. In 2015, Salzburg Global organized a session entitled "International Responses to Crimes Against Humanity: The Case of North Korea." The purpose of the program was to discuss and recommend practical ways by which outside actors—state and non-state as well as local, regional and global—might realistically aim to help improve the lot of the North Korean population. Participants included three members of the United Nations Commission of Inquiry on Human Rights in the Democratic People's Republic of Korea, together with human rights activists from around the world, government officials, research analysts, lawyers and journalists. At the conclusion of the program, participants produced a "Salzburg Statement" that summarized the issues discussed, and made recommendations for future action.

Although Salzburg Global Seminar enjoys an extremely unique venue for its seminars, in recent years programs have been held in various locations around the world, attended by Salzburg Global Fellows (alumni). In 2000 Salzburg Global began a series of seminars in partnership with Earth University, at its campus on Costa Rica's tropical Atlantic coast. The academic and commercial farms at Earth University comprise an extensive outdoor laboratory where vital hands-on learning takes place. Subsequent seminars in cooperation with Earth University took place in Thailand and Uganda in 2002, and Norway in 2003. In 2011, a two-day seminar was held in Moscow, called "Gaps in the Common Spaces: The Future of Russia-EU Relations." Attended by Salzburg Global Fellows, issues discussed included energy policy and the strong economic ties between Russia and the EU, since the EU is the largest market for Russian exports, and the EU was—at least in 2011—Russia's most important source of foreign investment. Also discussed was the move to regularize higher education across the region (the Bologna Process) and the on-going discussions concerning external security. In June 2012, a two-day seminar in Cairo was organized, entitled "Next Generation Leadership for Egypt." This followed a session in Salzburg in 2012 "The Challenges of Transition: Sharing Experience." The overthrow of former Egyptian president Hosni Mubarak signalized the desire of many Egyptians not only for a change of government but also for a generational change in the country's power structure. A new generation of leaders is waiting in the wings to effect change, and part of Salzburg Global Seminar's mission is to push developing leaders to meet challenges in collaboration with like-minded peers from around the world. The seminar was run in collaboration with the American University of Cairo, and capitalized on the networks of the AUC and Salzburg Global to focus on lessons for meeting challenges to progress in the public sector, the private sector and civil society.

Back in Salzburg, in August 2014, Salzburg Global Seminar and the International Peace Institute (IPI) brought together world leaders from politics, diplomacy, the media, and business along with historians, political scientists, artists and writers for the program "1814, 1914, 2014: Lessons from the Past, Visions for the Future." The topic seemed exceedingly timely, with rising instability around the world, and participants gathered to try to ascertain how lessons from the past could help restore public trust in the international system and in the ability of leaders to deliver solutions. One vision resulting from the program was the call for the establishment of a "Congress of the Middle East" given the major changes occurring in the region. Former Egyptian Foreign Minister Amre Moussa declared: "We need a plan worthy of the 21st century and a response to the needs and aspirations of the people" (Meduna 31). At the conclusion of the Salzburg Global-IPI program, IPI announced the establishment of the International Commission on Multilateralism (ICM). Chaired by one of the program participants, former Australian Prime Minister Kevin Rudd, and with eminent advisors such as Salzburg Global Senior Program Advisor Edward Mortimer, the ICM is a two-year process designed to analyze and make recommendations to strengthen the multilateral system.

Since 2011, Salzburg Global has convened an annual high-level forum focused on critical challenges of financial regulation following the global financial crisis. Called the "Forum on Finance in a Changing World," the program's goal is to facilitate critical analysis of the changing regularity environment, comparison of practical experience, and understanding of technology-driven transformations. Attendees are senior bankers, regulators, and policy makers from around the world—the United States, Asia and Europe, as well as international financial services firms, auditors and law firms. One recent fellow reported: "The level of the participants was incredible. I believe that no other place in the world can host such an array of high-ranking bankers, regulators, thinkers, and policymakers" (Hallman 2015: 36).

It is important to emphasize the decisive role played by the discipline of American studies in the development of the Salzburg Global Seminar over the past seventy years. During the Cold War, American studies programs at Schloss Leopoldskron provided a neutral site for dialogue, and the Salzburg Seminar continued to exist as a respected place to discuss important issues. Current American studies faculties and participants teach, communicate and interact with geographic multitudes of young people, future leaders and intellectuals. Over the last six decades, Salzburg Global Seminar has evolved into a global institution that brings together emerging and established global leaders to broaden thinking, challenge perspectives, enlarge horizons and lay the groundwork for future cooperation. Distinguished individuals such as Kofi Annan, former UN Secretary-General, and Paul Volcker, former Chairman of the Federal Reserve, have led discussions at Salzburg Global. Without adopting any political agenda of its own, Salzburg Global Seminar asks critical questions on the most pressing topics of our times—from climate change to the legacy of conflict, and from healthcare issues to trade barriers. Its ability to spark thought-provoking discussions, along with its serene setting, creates an environment where ideas matter, where differences are respected, and where those seeking a better world find common ground. It is a game-changing catalyst for international engagement, providing an international forum that cultivates meaningful connections, ground-breaking ideas and effective solutions to global challenges.

WORKS CITED

Eliot, Thomas H. and Lois H. Eliot. *The Salzburg Seminar*. Ipswich, MA: The Ipswich P, 1987.

Hallman, Louise, ed. *Salzburg Global Chronicle 2012-2013*. Salzburg: Salzburg Global Seminar, 2014.

—. *Salzburg Global Chronicle 2015*. Salzburg: Salzburg Global Seminar, 2015.

Matthiessen, F.O. *From the Heart of Europe.* New York: Oxford UP, 1948.

Meduna, Maximilian M. *1814, 1914, 2014: Lessons from the Past, Visions for the Future*. Salzburg: Salzburg Global Seminar, 2015.

Ryback, Timothy. "Encounters at the Schloss." *Harvard Magazine.* Nov.-Dec. (1987).

Salzburg Global Seminar. *Salzburg Global Vision – Imagination, Sustainability and Justice: The Power of Partnership*. Salzburg: Salzburg Global Seminar, 2013.

MOZART DIES INSTANTLY: CARL DJERASSI, *GRENZGÄNGER* BETWEEN THE UNITED STATES AND AUSTRIA

WALTER GRÜNZWEIG

Carl Djerassi is one of the most remarkable personalities of the twentieth, but also the twenty-first century. When he died on 29 January 2015, the media in many countries, including Austria, Germany and the United States, reported the passing away of a remarkable personality who, through his contributions to the development of the birth control pill, had had a major impact on human civilization. What made this scientist special was not only his achievements in chemistry, but also his ability to contextualize and interrogate this achievement, to understand its social and also cultural implications. Long before he became a novelist, a dramatist and a poet, he dealt with what he referred to as the "software" of his chemistry (Djerassi 1979: 1-5 and Djerassi 2001: 188-213), gauging the significance of his findings for societies not only in the developed world, the "geriatric" societies, as he liked to call them, but also for the developing "pediatric" countries (Djerassi 2014), which he knew well and which he perceived without western, or northern, prejudice.

From this concern for the soft dimensions of his scientific hardware, the decision to close his chemical laboratory and become a writer was logical, although it was neither small nor easy. His complaint that the natural sciences were "monological" led him to the "dialogical" character of literature (Djerassi 2000: x; Djerassi 2015: 243), and especially the theatre. He started his literary career on a pedagogical, almost didactic, note, arguing that he wanted to alleviate the scientific illiteracy of his readers. The lack of understanding—and also interest—in the sciences among the mass of readers of fiction was to be overcome by packing scientific knowledge into literary works, thus making it more palatable to the public. Until the end, Djerassi referred to this pedagogical impetus as a motivation for his writing, but this intentionalist approach, I believe, does not do full justice to his work (Djerassi 2015: 237; 244-45).

Already the sophisticated claim of the dialogicity of literature vis-à-vis the monological sciences went far beyond the notion of novels and plays as teaching tools. In fact, an exclusively pedagogical approach would have reduced the literary works to monological levels. But Djerassi's appreciation of deconstructive, post-structuralist notions of literature, which he learned from his wife, the eminent Stanford literary critic and biographer, Diane Middlebrook, and then fully embraced himself, made him understand literature not only as dialogical but as polyphonic and led him to question the limited epistemological basis of the natural sciences. Science-in-fiction, science-in-theatre, science-in-literature, were not just *representations* of the sciences and the scien*tist* in literature, but also demonstrated the discursive *constructions* of the sciences. This was done through the medium of literature, but the literary discourses transcended the works and became a part of the discursive analysis of the sciences.

He was, thus, a *Grenzgänger*, a wanderer between the sciences and literature, and this was not a leisurely walk but intellectual polygamy, as he liked to call it, with profound consequences for both. *Der intellektuelle Polygamist: Carl Djerassis Grenzgänge in Autobiographie, Roman und Drama*, the doctoral thesis by Graz Americanist Ingrid Gehrke, has demonstrated the interface between the sciences and literature in Djerassi's work at length (cf. Gehrke, especially 85-90; 213-23). Gehrke has also, in the words of Djerassi himself, through the analysis of his works, subjected him to a special kind of psychoanalysis which made him understand the relationship between his works and his biography. In a collection of essays entitled *The Sci-Artist: Carl Djerassi's Science-in-Literature in Transatlantic and Interdisciplinary Contexts*, the result of a 2009 symposium in Dortmund, the interdisciplinary, transgeneric dimension of his oeuvre was spatially and culturally extended by including a transatlantic dimension.

In the context of postwar cross-cultural encounters between the United States and Austria, a focus on Carl Djerassi as an Austrian-American scientist, writer and human being is called for. In various commentaries on the four honorary doctorates he has received in Austria and in many other places, much has been made of the Viennese birth of this remarkable personality, of his Jewish parents, both physicians, the mother Ashkenazy, the father Sephardic, who were more interested in their medical work than in their religion. When in 1938, at the age of sixteen, he and his mother had to make a quick escape from Vienna to save their lives, he was part of an intellectual mass exodus from which neither Austria, nor Central Europe, nor Germany, have ever recovered.

His scientific successes took place in the New World, in the Midwest, in Mexico, in California. For many years, he chose to ignore his Austrian origin and background. Probably he viewed his outstanding career early on as a version of a fortunate fall which he later frequently concretized as the good luck he had to get out of Vienna because had he remained there, he would "doubtless have ended up as an Austrian physician—possibly even one voting for Kurt Waldheim (Djerassi 2015 151).

But this almost complete, if temporary, oblivion regarding his Austrianness was to change radically with his emerging interest in literature and the dialogical mode. The development of his literary oeuvre and the re-discovery of his Austrian origins are intricately connected. An intense process of reflection led him to his remarkable return to Austria, the adoption of the city of his birth as a third place of residence, in addition to San Francisco and London—the latter becoming increasingly less important in his last years. With the beginning of a new, post-exilic Austrian life, Djerassi became an important, not just part, but embodiment, of the cross-cultural encounters between the United States and Austria.

It is obvious that post-war Austrian-American relations cannot be appreciated without consideration of the many Austrian exiles in the United States. The fact that Austria ignored them for a long time and that many of the exiles never returned, not even for a visit, does not mean that they are not a part of that history. Oftentimes, the German and Austrian view of exiles and their work is limited to the notion of loss—and thus to a Eurocentric perspective. In looking at these literary, artistic and intellectual losses and potentials, we are not primarily deploring those that have been driven out, but ourselves. The achievements, indeed the opportunities, of all of these tens of thousands of creative human beings in the countries and cultures that accepted them, are often not sufficiently respected. And the claim that their achievements in the new culture might also have been realized here in the old environment, is more than questionable.

The investigation of Austrian-American cross-cultural encounters must take into consideration the exiles' developments in their new environments. Such encounters are not only transatlantic phenomena but also occurred in the New World. An Austrian exile in the United States is a part of Austrian-American cultural relations. In Carl Djerassi, however, we have a very special case of an exile who did return—if late and only partially—and who involved himself actively, and sometimes pro-actively, in the public, artistic and political life of his country of origin. The fact that his case is very late and possibly also singular, does not reduce its importance. Neither does it take away from its paradigmatic significance, which calls for an inclusion of the Austrian exile in the United States in postwar history and evaluation of the cross-cultural relationships between the two countries.

In order to understand the gradual return of the exile to his country of origin and thus this Austrian-Americen encounter, I will look at Djerassi's autobiographical, but also literary, texts, some interviews and speeches, but will, of course, also bring in my own experience with him. This contribution cannot but be personal and, in fact, I do not want to hide my deep attachment to the man, which developed in the course of the almost two decades I knew him. Among the many exiles whose works I have written on and whom I have met personally, Carl Djerassi stands out. He has profoundly affected my own identity as an Austrian Americanist who grew up in the land of the perpetrators and who developed many, oftentimes escapist, strategies to disassociate himself from this context. In dialoguing with Djerassi, I also learned to understand and accept my own Austrianness and I believe this is an effect he had on many in this country who read him, who heard and saw him in the many television talk shows or encountered him in person.

When I first met Carl Djerassi in the second half of the 1990s—I have told this story in my obituary in the Austrian weekly magazine *profil*—I called my mother, three years older than Djerassi, for an idea of what we might serve this illustrious man for dinner. Strangely enough, she asked me his age and when I told her his birth year 1923, she suggested, for some reason, *Mohnnudeln,* the noodles made from potatoes with crushed poppy seeds and, of course, confectioner's sugar, *Staubzucker.* It turned out to be precisely the right choice. After the first couple of bites, Djerassi smiled at me and said: "With this dish, you have touched something that was deeply buried insided me" (Grünzweig 2015: 71).

Food, of course, connects an exile most easily to his origins when returning. "Vienna," he says in his fourth and last autobiography, *In Retrospect: From the Pill to the Pen*, "is my gustatory home, and that even the Nazis were not able to destroy" (Djerassi 2015: 130). In his first autobiography, *The Pill, Pygmy Chimps, and Degas' Horse* (1992), he writes in the initial chapter, entitled "Freud and I," about an early return to Austria with Diane Middlebrook who was presenting a paper at a conference on psychoanalysis and literature in 1988. Exactly fifty years earlier, on the fourth of July 1938, he writes—it is hard not to read this day symbolically—he had left Hitler's Vienna with his mother (Djerassi 1992: 5) The 1988 conference takes place in Kirchberg am Wechsel where, Djerassi does not know this at the time, Norbert Burger, *Südtirol-Bumser* and founder of the

Austrian neonazi party NPD, lives, the very same Burger who had received 140,000 votes in the Austrian presidential elections eight years earlier.

> Arriving at our *Gasthof*, we sit down for lunch. The choices in our small inn are limited to various *Schnitzel.* At the sight of my *Naturschnitzel mit Champignons,* drowned in cream sauce, the Viennese in me salivates, even as the weight-conscious, lipophobic Californian draws back in horror. I assuage my calorie guilt complex by deciding to behave abstemiously at dinner. After a few hours of deep sleep, we stroll to the restaurant where the other visiting academics are assembled, to face the second Austrian menu of the day. "No main dish," I proclaim to my wife in a voice full of virtuousness, "just soup and modest dessert." I should have known better, but I had not been back to Austria for a long time: "just" and "modest"—at least in matters culinary—have a very different meaning in this country. The soup is *Leberknödel Suppe*, which I, born with a soupspoon in my mouth, have not tasted for decades. Attacking the huge liver dumpling, I rediscover Archimedes' principle: I have consumed hardly half the *Knödel* when I find the remaining broth barely covering the bottom of the soup plate. Culinary symmetry and gustatory nostalgia lead me to choose *Germknödel* for dessert. *Knödel*, the German word for "dumpling," has no plural, like *sheep* in English. Since my departure from Vienna in 1938, I have tasted on occasion *Marillenknödel* or *Zwetschgenknödel*—small dessert dumplings stuffed with apricots or plums; but my last *Germknödel* dates back to the pre-*Anschluss* days. I have forgotten that this comes as one giant *Knödel*, squatting over the entire plate, generously freckled with poppy seeds, drenched in butter, and, most delectable, stuffed with *Powidl*, the Austrian plum jam. In California, I would have gone on a four-day fast to make up for this megacoloric sin, but here, in Kirchberg am Wechsel, instead of sinking like a stone to the bottom of my stomach, the first bite of the *Germknödel* immediately penetrates my blood-brain barrier. Like a crack smoker after the first puff, I experience an instant high. (Djerassi 1992: 6)

Just as in the case of my later *Mohnnudeln,* the taste evokes an immediate connection to a past experience deep inside him which is recovered. At the same time, however, there is something threatening about this food which overwhelms him. The two sides of his personality, the Californian and the Viennese, are far from being reconciled. "My childhood memory has become a dusty lens, the focus poor, the picture patchy" (Djerassi 1992: 13). When, after eating Austrian in Graz, Trieste and Berlin and other places, the two of us had what turned out to be our last meal together in the fall 2014 in the very Viennese Gmoakeller, Djerassi ordered *Fritattensuppe* and *Hirn mit Ei,* a soup with pancake strips followed by what in the U.S. would be "soul food," brains with eggs. In his eating, he was about as Viennese as one could get.

The next-to-last chapter of the 1992 autobiography is entitled "Return to Vienna: 'Wien, Wien, nur Du allein....'' His first autobiography is thus framed by two Austrian chapters whereas the main body rarely refers to the city and the country of his birth. The latter chapter has Carl and his son Dale briefly visit Vienna on the layover of a flight between San Francisco and the Maldives:

> The weather is balmy this late October 1989, and many people sit in outdoor cafés or stroll in typical late Saturday afternoon fashion. Suddenly, we come upon two musicians, a violinist and a cellist, who are surrounded by quiet, almost reverential onlookers. With a flourish of his bow, the violinist starts a highly professional rendition of Mozart's *Eine kleine Nachtmusik.* (Djerassi 1992: 298)

What amounts to the writer's "Vienna-bred sentimentality," however, is suddenly dispelled: "my emotional house of cards collapses" (Djerassi 1992: 299). Three tall policemen—"tall and not yet potbellied"

> [...] walk straight through the listeners' cordon, which opens like a cell being penetrated by an invading virus. The tallest of the cops stalks toward the violinist, getting so close to him as to force him to glance up from the music stand. Mozart dies instantly. (Djerassi 1992: 299)

The—American—biological metaphor enters the Austrian idyll which self-destructs. The typology between 1938 and 1989 represented by the intervention of the policeman demonstrates that the rapprochement to or with Austria will not be easy. Mozart dies instantly, leaving the Californians to cope with a very difficult situation and, in terms of the autobiographical narrative, voiding the retrogressive culinary utopia of the first chapter. The chapter ends with an extremely ambivalent impression: "Past overfed *Loden*-clad burghers gorging themselves with *Schlag*-covered cakes and coffee, my son and I walk on, each in his own way struck dumb" (Djerassi 1992: 299).

His return to Vienna was truly a long process. Djerassi liked to emphasize that up into the mid-1990s, there were only three European countries from which he had never received an invitation to lecture on chemical topics, small entities such as San Marino excluded: Albania, Portugal and Austria. Although he claimed that he realized that it was foolish to expect any special treatment, he also admitted that this lack of recognition bothered him (Djerassi 2015: 109-10). But instead of giving up on Austria and concentrate on his success in the rest of the world, like many of his fellow exiles, he embarked on a remarkable dialogue with his country of origin which amounts to a programmatic effort.

His literary works were early on translated into German, sometimes even before the publication in the original English. But Austria had little to do with it. His first publisher, Haffmans, was Swiss, and his translator, Ulrike Mössner, was German. Djerassi points out that his own rediscovery of the German language and his reception in German went through Germany rather than Austria. It required, he says, a translator with a "modern German voice [...] and a woman's voice at that to bring me to terms with my European origins" (Djerassi 2015: 111).

The fact that he received an Austrian passport—it was not a case of a restitution of his citizenship because it turned out that he had always retained his father's Bulgarian citizenship—seems to have been more a matter of convenience, allowing him and his wife to travel and reside more comfortably in Europe. The reason given by the officials, namely that "the bestowal of citizenship is based on the already realized as well as the still anticipated extraordinary achievements in the special interest of the Republic [of Austria]" (Djerassi 2015: 119-20), did not impress him given the fact that the Austrian Republic obviously offered a deal formulating further expectations.

What truly seems to have changed his relationship to Austria was that the Austrian postal authorities issued a stamp on his behalf in 2005. In a special session of the American Chemical Society in San Francisco, I once used three Austrian stamps featuring three Austrian-Americans as a starting point. Charles Sealsfield, self-exiled nineteenth-century Austrian writer of America novels, Arnold Schwarzenegger and, of course, Carl Djerassi. Djerassi, who did not quite know what to make of this philatelistic neighborhood, reacted quickly and in a clever way: "But I," he said, "am the only one who returned." The stamp provided the language for Djerassi to explain his emerging new relationship with Vienna and Austria.

Presenting him as both "*Chemiker*" and "*Romancier*"—Chemist and novelist—his relationship with Austria is summarized in three particular years and three words:

> "*1923: Geboren, 1938: Vertrieben, 2003: Versöhnt.*"
> Born in 1923, expelled in 1938, reconciled in 2003.

The term "*versöhnt*," "reconciled," is key here. It does not mean forgiveness and certainly not forgetting, as he himself reminded many of his Austrian audiences. The etymology is significant, both for the German term and the English. The frequently assumed *Volksetymologie* referring "*versöhnt*" to "*Sohn*" (son) is wrong, the word used to be "*versühnen*" and is related to "*Sühne*," atonement. Both in the Jewish and the Christian tradition, "*Versöhnung*" requires an acknowledgement of sin and guilt before this process can set in. The etymology of the English word, reconciliation, to bring together once more, implies the event of separation and therefore also requires a reflection of the causes of this separation. Linguistically, the word "*versöhnt*" provides agency to the exile. Just as he was born—*geboren*—as he was expelled—*vertrieben*—he is now reconciled—*versöhnt*—as a result of his own willingness to reconciliate. His earlier quoted statement that the Austrian Republic and her institutions had not reached out to him expresses disappointment. Through his decision to become reconciled, to reach out to his land and his city of birth, he not only begins a process which might never have started otherwise, he also puts himself into a strategically favorable position as *he* is the one to decide the terms and the conditions upon which this process is taking place. Normally, the symbolic value of a stamp recognizes the accomplishments by an outstanding personality. The state, represented by the postal authorities, elects to honor somebody for achievements defined by the state as being relevant. Here, the personality's achievements are referred to, it is primarily an expression of the recognition of a moral responsibility on the part of the issuing country.

This is a pattern which can be recognized in subsequent interactions between Djerassi and Vienna or Austria. Whereas it was a process that was obviously initiated by his autobiographical and fictional/dramatic work (Djerassi calls his literary work his "true autobiography"), it is also specifically related to his emerging interest in the Jewish tradition which he claimed to never have been truly interested in earlier. In 1999, I wrote an article on Djerassi for Vienna's *Das Jüdische Echo* which I subtitled: "A Jew and intellectual bigamist." I looked at the many Jewish protagonists of his works, mostly deeply secular scientists, who are nevertheless identified as Jews, if only through their names (Grünzweig 1999: 247-50). Martin Buber calls the essence of Judaism "dialogical"—not surprising for a thinker who has put dialogue into center of his philosophy—and it is easy to see the connection between Buber's and Djerassi's emphasis on dialogue.

The protagonist of Djerassi's first and most famous novel *Cantor's Dilemmna*, his satire—and/or criticism—of the nobel prize as an institution, is Isidore Cantor, in short "I.C." He is a world-renowned American cancer researcher and thus a scientist in body and soul. But he also leads a kind of double life as an art collector (Schiele and Vienna Jugendstil furniture) and musician. His father-in-law was a Jewish exile from Vienna who, shortly before the *Anschluss*, managed to escape Vienna with all of his property which facilitated Cantor's career as a collector (Djerassi 2009: 21). At least in part, his scientific approaches are also informed by aesthetic perception. Cantor's student, Stafford, says that his mentor is able to "synthesize concepts from a few isolated observations" (Djerassi 1991: 79)—an intuitive, creative, aesthetic approach.

But Isidore Cantor is also, as his name shows, Jewish or at least of Jewish origin, although this fact is not further elaborated on in the book. The name is there and that is sufficient: the cantor of a Jewish congregation is a mediator between God and the believers. He speaks and sings the prayers. In his dialogical approach between the sciences and the arts, "I.C." has a similar function.

The secular Jews in Djerassi's novels—the majority of his protagonists are hinted at as being Jewish, though no more—are literary anticipations of his docudrama *Four Jews on the Parnassus* (2008). In both Djerassi's (and my own) view, it is his most important book, especially because of his very happy encounter with Salzburg artist Gabriele Seethaler who created the art on which its effect depends. In bringing together leading Jewish intellectuals and artists of the twentieth century—Adorno, Benjamin, Scholem and Schönberg—on Mount Parnassus, this book presents a "foursome" of "German and Austrian bourgeois Jews of the pre-World War II generation who often were more Berliners or Viennese than their non-Jewish compatriots" (Djerassi 2008: xv).

> This is also the generation and social subset to which I belong, and my personal experience with the indelible effects of growing up as secular Jew in Vienna in the 1930s made me want to examine the range of the meaning of *Jew* through four individuals who responded so differently to that label. (Djerassi 2008: xv)

Thus, the process of reconciliation was connected to a new dimension, that of his Jewishness, which he had never consciously reflected when in Vienna—or afterwards—but which is now important in his step-by-step return. To avoid misunderstandings, Djerassi was not at all religious. When I suggested to him that for example the complexity and fascination of his own work makes me doubt that everything in life is coincidental and want to believe in an agency of order and control in the universe, he merely sneered. The only thing that can be lasting—maybe—he said, is reputation. So the Jewishness to be investigated and taken into consideration was cultural, but it did add an important dimension in his reconciliation with Austria. It was a part of the new terms with which he encountered the country he had been driven from.

Following his wife Diane Middlebrook's death in 2007, Djerassi connected the question of how to organize his life with geographical decisions. In a long phone call shortly after her death he explained to me that he would need a culturally charged environment in Europe, preferably German-speaking, in order to be able to go on. His sense of loss was extreme and he felt that European urban environments would help him. Specifically, he singled out Berlin and Vienna and even test-lived in Berlin at first. I soon realized, however, that he would end up in Vienna, because there he had an agenda, namely that of the reconciliation with the city of his birth on his own terms.

In the preparation of a TV talk show in 2010, Djerassi was asked to explain his notions of "*Heimat*," a term he emphasized is hard to translate into English. A translation with the lexical monster "homeland," which entered the bureaucratic-paranoid American language after 2001, is certainly not adequate. "*Heimat*," to Djerassi, then was what he had lost in 1938 and which he would never get back. It is not necessarily connected with identity; indeed, a "homeless identity" is preferable. "*Heimat*" is a highly subjective term, although many people misjudge it as objective. Globalization, at least for Djerassi, does not strengthen the significance of "*Heimat*." Eventually, one can acquire a personal, virtual "*Heimat*," which has nothing to do with one's place of birth (Djerassi 2015: 134-139).

Thus, Djerassi frankly rejected any notion of "*Heimat*" with regard to his move back to Vienna. What he lost, he had lost in 1938 and it could not be recovered, at least not through a sense of place: "If you are kicked out of your country, you can never get it back" (Djerassi 2012b). Returning home would be re-entering the culture on the old terms, which is impossible. What does happen, rather, is the establishment of a new relationship, or relationships, *based* on the old, which allows the exile to face his country on equal terms.

In a speech on the occasion of the seventieth anniversary of the *Anschluss*, on 11 November 2008, at the Philologisch-Kulturwissenschaftliche Fakultät in Vienna, he stated this carefully:

> The true motivation for a natural born Viennese who was expelled in 1938 and who then turned into an American, was the possibility to speak with a Vienna audience of our time, 70 years after the horrific Anschluss, about my present feelings *vis-à-vis* my place of birth. (Djerassi 2009: 15; all translations from this publication are mine, WG)

Whereas a representative of the Vienna Medical School, Horst Aspöck, magnanimously thanked Djerassi "for having become Viennese again," ("[…] *wir danken Ihnen von ganzem Herzen, dass Sie wieder Wiener geworden sind,*" Djerassi 2009: 14), he is choosing to address a Viennese public on the relationship with his place of birth. Djerassi continues:

> For me, this is important and for you maybe of interest, as I found out almost twenty years ago that after a half a century of life as an American my European roots had not completely dried up and that watering these roots by nostalgic reflexes stimulated new growth which then even started to grow all kinds of new shoots ("Sprosse"). (Djerassi 2009: 15)

The emphasis is on his own interest and his audience will be well-advised not to fall into a state of nostalgic forgetfulness. Rather, the semi-ironic "nostalgic reflexes" are merely the water which facilitate new growth in all sorts of ways and directions.

One of these shoots is Djerassi's Austrian play, *Phallacy* (German: *Phallstricke*), in which the authenticity of a famous sculpture in the Vienna Museum of Art History, the "Youth of Magdalensberg," is questioned. It turns out that though it is indeed the copy of a Roman statue, it is a sixteenth-century cast. Aesthetically, it is thus Roman, as the art historian in the play emphasizes; materially, it is not, as the chemist correctly states. Whether the art historian or the chemist, aesthetics or hard science, makes the more relevant statement is less important than the inextricable ambivalence which remains and must be accepted—and is actually transcended by the recognition that the work of art has become part of the global canon of human artistic achievement. With this play, Djerassi virtually produced an allegory of his own situation between his origin and his later life.

The fact that Djerassi ends his speech on a very critical note shows that he is not willing to give in to foul nostalgia-ridden compromises. Pointing to the sharp rise of the votes for the right-wing Austrian "Freedom Party" (FPÖ) and Jörg Haider's BZÖ party in the elections of 2008, Djerassi reflected on the large success for Austrian parties which are xenophobic (Djerassi 2009: 33-34). He was irritated "not only for moral reasons but also because this documents a stupid attitude" (Djerassi 2009: 34).

> Obviously, almost 30% of the inhabitants of this country have been trained in schools that do not teach anything about the demographic situation of our current world. These Austrians are still victims of the illusion that their small country is not located in the center of Europe but on a small island where God allows them to live entirely in isolation from the rest of the world to enjoy their *Beuschel*, *Marillenknödel* and *Schlag*. (Djerassi 2009: 34)

What he targets is the Austrian (and, incidentally, German) shortsightedness not to recognize the necessity of migration to Austria given the inevitable population decline. "As Viennese American—or American Viennese—I consider it my task to emphasize the hardly ever verbalized implications of the results of the last elections" (Djerassi 2009: 39). By quoting from statements by the *Burschenschaft* fraternity of Martin Graf, erstwhile president of the Austrian parliament, namely that the "infiltration of the

German people by members of foreign peoples threatens the biological and cultural substance of the German people" (Djerassi 2009: 39), he takes a strong stand using his unique insights into demographic developments, an exile's bold intervention in his country of origin.

The speaker at the Viennese Philologisch-Kulturwissenschaftliche Fakultät stated at the end of his welcome that "Carl Djerassi had the greatness to offer forgiving and reconciliation" (Djerassi 2009: 13). Commenting on his stamp in his last autobiography, however, Djerassi stated in what could be considered his final words: "I have always made it plain that 'reconcile' does not mean 'forgive' or 'forget,' but it does mean moving forward" (2015: 145) Who or what is moving forward is not specified here. Life, of course, but also the process of reconciliation.

And it is here that he brings in his most amazing move vis-à-vis Austria, his gifts of art to the Austrian people: "To reaffirm this personal belief"—namely that reconciliation is neither forgetting nor forgiving, "a few years after my Rickey gift [a George Rickey sculpture to Vienna], I decided to transfer to the [Vienna] Albertina one half of my large Paul Klee collection with the other half passing to the San Francisco Museum of Modern Art" (Djerassi 2015: 145-46). There is, of course, in the division of the collection, which nevertheless belongs together, a symbol of the divided situation of the collector. But in the Vienna context, Viennese-born Djerassi is leaving a significant mark in one of the central locations of Viennese and Austrian culture.

That this mark is Paul Klee is symbolic, even though it was of course not intended as such from the beginning of his passion for collecting this artist. The activity of collecting, gathering and holding on to things, says Djerassi, is an activity to fill a void (Djerassi 2013), and thus a characteristic activity of an exile. Collecting Klee relates the collector to his own experiences of this fatal twentieth century, but is also a way to deal with its dislocations aesthetically. In *Four Jews on Parnassus,* Djerassi connects Klee with visions of this fatal history and the notion of history itself. In a dialog with me on Klee's poetry published in *Der Standard*, Djerassi emphasized Klee's biographical relevance—also for himself (Djerassi and Grünzweig 2002).

Carl Djerassi's slow, contradictory but consistent return to Austria amounts to a program which is yet to unfold. The works, the donations, the many literary and cultural inscriptions, represent an exile's strategy of coping with loss which is open-ended and actually charts out the future also of

Austrian-American encounters which can never be separated from the experience of exile.

WORKS CITED

Djerassi, Carl. *The Politics of Contraception.* New York, London: Norton, 1979.
—. *Cantor's Dilemma. A Novel.* New York: Penguin, 1991.
—. *An Immaculate Misconception. Sex in an Age of Mechanical Reproduction.* London: Imperial College P, 2000.
—. *This Man's Pill. Reflections on the 50th Birthday of the Pill.* Oxford: Oxford UP, 2001.
—. *Four Jews on Parnass: A Conversation. Benjamin, Adorno, Scholem, Schönberg.* Illustrations by Gabriele Seethaler. New York: Columbia UP, 2008.
—. *Nach 70 Jahren: Wiener Amerikaner oder amerikanischer Wiener?* Göttingen: V&R unipress (Vienna UP), 2009.
—. *Chemistry in Theatre: Insufficiency, Phallacy, or Both.* London: Imperial College P, 2012a.
—. "Ich wollte sehen, ob meine Muttersprache zu mir zurückkehrt." Interview with Thomas Keul (2012b). Web. 2012.
—. "Vom Füllen der Leere." Interview with Walter Grünzweig. *Der Standard* 20/21 April 2013.
—. "Unbefleckt zum Wunschkind. Sex im Zeitalter der technologischen Reproduktion." *Neue Zürcher Zeitung* 24 Sept. 2014.
—. *In Retrospect: From the Pill to the Pen.* London: Imperial College P, 2015.
Djerassi, Carl and Walter Grünzweig. "Das Ich als dramatisches Ensemble." *Der Standard* 8 June 2002.
Gehrke, Ingrid. *Der intellektuelle Bigamist: Carl Djerassis Grenzgänge in Autobiographie, Roman und Drama.* Münster, Berlin: Lit, 2008.
Grünzweig, Walter. "Carl Djerassi, Vater der Pille: Ein Jude als intellektueller Bigamist." *Das Jüdische Echo* 48 (1999): 244-50.
— (ed.). *The SciArtist: Carl Djerassi's Science-in-Literature in Transatlantic and Interdisciplinary Contexts.* Münster, Berlin: Lit, 2012.
—. "Der intellektuelle Polygamist." *Profil*, 9 Feb. 2015, 70-72.

The Image of Home Lost (and Rediscovered): Walter Abish and William H. Gass Writing the Austrian Past

Marta Koval

> Tanta vis admonitionis inest in locis. (Great is the power of memory that resides in places.)
>
> Cicero, *De finibus bonorum et malorum*

The problematic of memory in today's literary and cultural studies includes a variety of concepts and approaches that combine textuality with lived experience. Quite often, places, objects and events respectively constituting the setting and plot of the memorial narrative become texts in their own right, laden, as it were, with significant emotional charges. They do not just exist as neutral elements of a frame of reference, but function as repositories of the author's dynamic identity. As Aleida Assmann notes in *Cultural Memory and Western Civilization*,

> The expression "the memory of places" is both convenient and evocative. It is convenient because it leaves open the question of whether this is *genetivus objectivus*, meaning that we remember places, or a *genetivus subjectivus*, meaning that places retain memories. It is evocative because it suggests the possibility that places themselves may become the agents and bearers of memory, endowed with a mnemonic power that far exceeds that of humans. (281)

Double Vision (2004), an essay-memoir by Walter Abish, and *Middle C* (2013), the most recent novel by William H. Gass, are texts about a lost home in a broader or narrower sense of the word that can also be read as narratives about places that remember and, conversely, places that are remembered. The image of Austria as a cultural icon and a nostalgic object is created in both works by two models of memory. Even though both belong to the category of inhabited memory (Assmann's term), their essential features differ in terms of dealing with the past.

In the "Austrian" part of *Double Vision* Abish brings together fragments of memories of his early childhood in Vienna in the 1930s before the *Anschluss*. The memoir reveals a double perspective implied by its title: warm and slightly sentimental memories from the pre-war times mix with keen and critical observations about present-day Vienna. In this portrait of the city artistic urbanism merges with personal memories linked to the place. A naïve child's perspective is imposed on a vision of a mature individual and a well-established and experienced writer, no longer an Austrian, but a cosmopolitan American. As a result, a nostalgic and atmospheric urban image is marked, on the one hand, by child-like amazement and on the other, the disappointment of a mature individual caused by Austria's political conformism that is paradoxically merged with an irresistible charm of the city.

Abish, now a famous American writer, returns to Vienna, the city of his childhood, presumably in the late 1980s. He does not specify the year of his visit but the reader can guess it on the basis of publication dates of Thomas Bernhard's novels to which Abish refers extensively. As the writer claims, he comes to Vienna without any particular expectations—just out of curiosity in order to verify if the city created by his memory and invoking a "misleading intimacy" would be in any way familiar so many years later. However, the epigraph to the "contemporary" (as opposed to the mnemonic) part of the Austrian story begins with a quotation from Bernhard that explicitly and unambiguously speaks of a wish to revisit the past and a pain of not finding it: "I walk along Mariahilferstrasse / looking for Mariahilferstrasse / I'm on Mariahilferstrasse / and I can't find it" (Abish 107). In his observations of Vienna, Abish will often turn to Bernhard—apparently one of his favorite writers, who added yet another rather perverse perspective of the city that was important for both of them. For Abish a new understanding of Vienna would not be possible without a retrospective contemplation of his earlier experience of the place. Thus, the Austrian part of the memoir is a perfect example of the "archeology of metropolis" (the expression frequently used in the contemporary cultural studies)—an open and emotional exploration of the city as it used to be and as it is at present.

The memories of Abish's early childhood in Vienna are mainly episodes of family life—manners, habits, customs, relations, wishes and minor misfortunes. The atmosphere of the city as a specific existential space is created predominantly by its residents. A slow and well-balanced pace of pre-war Viennese life molds their characters and fills their everyday existence with tranquility and their homes with order, predictability, and an overriding need for bodily comfort, which Walter as a child did not fail to notice: "On the walls several still lifes and bleak landscapes in heavy gilded frames. There's nothing decorative or frivolous about them. They look serious. I now realize that their function was to signify not art but normality" (Abish 18). The writer's childhood memories, although not always pleasant, are generally warm and sentimental. The reader plunges into the atmosphere of urban homeyness created by stereoscopic glimpses of city life where the urban merges with the personal so that the city eventually becomes a larger home:

> There was little in the house—my mother's domain—that held his [Abish's father's] attention. He preferred the tranquility of his beloved Viennese cafes, these cozy retreats where he could read his newspapers and journals undisturbed. I suspect that the cafes ranked second in importance only to his business, to his treasured perfumes—those tiny, elegantly shaped bottles snugly encased in their pale yellow boxes bearing the name Molinard as well as their poetic fragrances. (Abish 7)

At a certain moment, memories of the writer's childhood in Vienna lose their linear coherence and become a mosaic of charming and emotionally colorful retrospective glimpses of the city and its people. In Abish's memories, streets, buildings, parks and the population are equally important and complementary. The tragic events of March 1938 caused by Hitler's annexation of Austria are presented through the images of everyday urban life and Viennese residents' changed behavior without extensive political comments. The American writer Walter Abish, involved in a classic autobiographical paradox of the split which separates the teller now and then, tries to reconstruct and describe what little Walter, for whom the Jewishness of his family did not mean or matter much, could feel while observing "the almost ritualized humiliation inflicted on the Viennese Jews" (Abish 23). He admits that as a child he remained in complete ignorance of the political change, though he felt unmistakably that his familiar and predictable world collapsed. Now, under completely different circumstances, he tries to conceptualize this change: "Overnight my familiar world was defamiliarized. Could this be the origin of my fascination with the quotidian – the familiar everyday world?" (25). The city transformed rapidly together with political realities. The atmosphere of tranquility and happy nonchalance embodied by the image of the *Pischkotentorte*, "that triumph of Viennese pastries" on the kitchen table which Walter noticed as a child when the family was forced to vacate the apartment, disappears with no hope for return. Apparently, a small, embittered and upset child was quite unable to explain that almost apocalyptic change. As an adult author, Abish does it though from the perspective of his younger self—lost, upset and overwhelmed by the inexplicable. The cityscape turns into a theater where a low-quality and vulgar performance is given to a reluctant audience. The narrator seems to remember more about a few months of 1938 than about his entire childhood in Vienna, since what is colored by strong emotions is always remembered best:

> [T]he streets of Vienna took on the appearance of a staged spectacle —one of those beloved operettas that skirt reality—for the frenzied, flag-waving Viennese did not merely proclaim their solidarity with Germany and embrace their Austrian-born Hitler; rather, they embraced the Anschluss, seizing the opportunity to display those tantalizing new emblems, the paraphernalia of Nazism, and in a state of exuberance perform a celebratory dance. A heady performance. How invigorating to be able to dress up! That's what it took to become a Nazi. A breathless encounter, as the Viennese—whose dialect, after all, is replete with double meanings—absorbed with a shudder of ecstasy the aesthetics of the swastika. Vienna—dying and fading Vienna—temporarily invigorated. (Abish 26)

The German words used to describe the realities of life in Abish's Vienna (in *Double Vision* these are mainly names of dishes) not only recreate a specific atmosphere of urban chic and "normality." They also function as stabilizers of memory (Assmann's term) that help to recall objects and facts as well as reconstruct a specific group's conventions and ways of thinking. [1]

Abish's return to Vienna in the 1980s was not a nostalgic trip. Rather, it was an attempt to see how important the Viennese fragment of the past still

[1] According to Assmann, language is the most powerful stabilizer of memory. She claims that "whatever we have captured in language is far easier to remember than something that has never been articulated." In addition to language, Assmann singles out other psychic stabilizers of memory, such as affect, symbol and trauma. With various degrees of intensity, these "translate" physical experience into "meaning" (239). Abish uses all of them, although language is obviously the most functional.

was and to view oneself "in a different light, in an Austrian context" (Abish 108). Although Abish is aware that the charming intimacy of Vienna is misleading and he speaks of the city in the language of an experienced traveler, he still feels at home there: "I felt as if I was resuming a conversation I'd left off some time before" (110). According to Svetlana Boym, being at home is a state of mind that does not depend on an actual location but implies that things are in their places and so are you (251). Abish notices the way people are dressed and the way they speak—the "rich, pliant Viennese language enabling [...] to shift back and forth from irony to seeming candor, from self-deprecation to ridicule" and "the melodious Viennese" with "an odd mix of humor and understatement" (Abish 109-10). But mostly he keeps looking for what he seems to remember well—the house at Königseggasse 2 where he was born and raised, and buildings along Mariahilferstrasse he once used to walk along with his father. They are recognizable and at the same time completely foreign, as in Bernhard's sentence "I'm on Mariahilferstrasse / and I can't find it." Abish's description of the house in Königseggasse brings into play the idea of the specific aura of places of memory. For Walter Benjamin, such places were "a strange tissue of space and time: the unique apparition of distance, however near it may be" (Benjamin 14). According to Benjamin, the aura of places is not based on directness or closeness. On the contrary, it implies remoteness, strangeness and unapproachability. In her explanation of this concept, Assmann emphasizes that an "auratic place in this sense does not promise an unmediated experience; it is, rather, a place where the unbridgeable gap between present and past can be experienced" (322). The streets and buildings that remember Abish as a little boy imply the idea of "here and then" (Assmann's concept as an opposition to the idea of "here without a now"):

> Though the house in all respects resembled the house in which I had spent the first years of my life, it also, in some indefinable way, failed to do so. Examining it carefully, I searched my memories, if only to extract from my past some detail to illuminate this long-delayed return. At length, mildly unsettled, unable to activate any strong emotional response, I walked away—only to return for another look. Finally, almost dutifully, I photographed it from several angles. If anything, I experienced a satisfaction at feeling so indifferent. It was just another house! (Abish 111)

Such places of individual memory bring together "sensual presence and historical absence" (Assmann 322) and their aura is defined by their alienation, which Abish's surprised and even disappointed "It was just another house!" expresses in a more than obvious way.

Buildings do not have the innate faculty of memory, as Assmann observes, but they are very important for the construction of cultural memory: "Not only do they stabilize and authenticate the latter by giving it a concrete setting, but they also embody continuity, because they outlast the relatively short spans of individuals, eras, and even cultures and their artifacts" (Assmann 282). Thus for Abish the house in Königseggasse is a complex emotional and psychological construction: on one hand, it functions as a link to the past—both personal (the sweet time of childhood) and national (Vienna's glorious and shameful history). On the other, as Abish admits, the actual house does not invoke any strong sentiments. It was expected to speak the language of nostalgia but did not. Even though memories turn it into a convenient frame of reference, the city's past by no means determines its present but only adds some sentimental notes to its reading. All the places of memory persistently keep "here and then" apart.

Childhood memories merge with the actual present and are imposed on it: the place remembered transforms into the place that remembers and then the categorical gap between "here and then" disappears. The buildings that Abish sees lived a life of their own without the observer who is trying to find in them the traces of his past life. However, despite the effort, the buildings themselves feel alienated and emotionally empty. The atmosphere of familiarity is created exclusively by people, manners, the pace of life, and the unchanged cultural frame of meaning which Abish savors with an apparent visual and verbal pleasure and a slight touch of nostalgic longing:

> Sitting at one of the round marble-topped tables at the nearby Café Aida—had it always been in that very site?—I observed a matronly-looking lady who minutes earlier had arrived by taxi and now, with motions of practiced refinement, was fastidiously consuming two Viennese specialties: first a generous portion of Apfelstrudel, followed by an elaborate concoction of chocolate smothered in whipped cream. A familiar world? How could it not be? Even her tiny felt hat, worn at an angle, a small rectitudinous fortification intended to discourage all advances, marked her Viennese respectabil-

> ity and virtue. I ordered another grosser Brauner. A familiar world? One could slip into it so easily. (110-11)

Step by step it becomes obvious that the writer's private memories of the place irrevocably belong to the past. What Abish admires and what matters for him is the Vienna of the present that carries the imprints of its painful history which nonetheless do not affect its character. This approach may be identified as the functional component of the narrator's inhabited memory. It is conscious remembrance that implies a particular configuration of meaning: "The life story that one 'inhabits' ties together memories and experiences in a narrative construction of the self that determines one's life and provides guidance for future actions" (Assmann 124). At a certain point, Abish's admiration of the city and the willingness with which he plunges into its life become only very loosely linked to his personal story. He speaks of Vienna as if it were a living creature—beautiful, melancholic, sweet and hedonistic: "An unruffled and calm, if not serene, world. One could easily spend hours in the cafes. The city was full of agreeable, out-of-the-way retreats that offered Gemütlichkeit. Comfort was uppermost in the minds of the Viennese" (Abish 111). As the writer jokes, one can drown in Vienna's melancholic "sweetness"—that was what made Bernhard resist the city so forcefully and what Abish as an outsider finds luring. Under the irresistible influence of the city's charm, his childhood memories lose their significance because the "city imagines its future by improvising on its past" (Abish 75) and not by living in it. The beauty of Vienna that arose over history overshadows personal trauma, while improvisation implies freedom of interpretation and expression. Walking in the Belvedere, Abish feels "like a participant in a staged event, a timeless occurrence, for everything in Belvedere's exuberant design seemed as vital as the day it was constructed by Hildebrandt and Girard. Everything, from the remoteness to the alluring symmetry, annunciates taste—taste that stands supreme" (117-18). Places like that undoubtedly "witnessed" and "remembered" many events and people, but those memories are in fact insignificant because life in Vienna is governed by well-measured and timeless beauty. The trials of history lose their meaning and failures of the past disperse because the city feels like "a soft, inviting bed with an eiderdown blanket" encouraging a visitor to take a nap that might just as well last a lifetime: "One need only scan the entertaining but utterly trivial articles on the court life of Maria Theresa or Franz Joseph in *Die Presse*, written as if they were present-day events, to become aware that the terror of history didn't lie heavily on this city—it was merely a convenient frame of reference" (Abish 120). Thus, a visit to the city that could have been an encounter with the past turned into an encounter with beauty which took over history. However, one can still say that the image of Vienna in Abish's memoir is shaped both by beauty and history, each determining one's understanding of the other. The beauty of the city would be less impressive and meaningful without the awareness of its glorious and painful past, not dominating the reading of Vienna but ever-present in it, whereas the past would be more difficult to bear but for the city's beauty. An American writer of Austrian origin is probably the most likely—thanks to distance in time, space and culture—to realize that ambiguity.

Memory is also a prism through which Austria is seen in William H. Gass's most recent novel, *Middle C*. Here, however, the reader is given an emotionally and psychologically different image of Austria that derives from a different attitude towards the Austrian past. In Abish's memoir, a self-conscious work of nonfiction, the latter is multidimensional and thus inspiring. For one central character in *Middle C*, it is determined by nostalgia that turns out to be unproductive and restrictive.

Gass creates a typical idealized image of the Austrian province that Nita/Miriam Skizzen, mother of the protagonist Joseph Skizzen, cherishes and takes to the United States. For this character in Gass's novel, nostalgia is closely linked to her small *Heimat*, the town of Graz. Simple and idyllic life in Austria becomes even more idealized over time and the fact that Miriam never revisits her home country helps her maintain the image of a romantic past that most probably has little to do with the reality of an American life filled with hard work, anxiety for survival, and the incomprehensible values of a society of immigrants with different ethnic and cultural backgrounds. Miriam's nostalgia for her Austrian home as "a mourning for the impossibility of mythical return, for the loss of an enchanted world with clear borders and values" (Boym 8) is so strong that it becomes part of her identity-making.

When the Second World War broke out, Nita/Miriam, who was Austrian, was forced by her husband not only to leave her home country and the town of Graz, but also to change her identity. Rudi Skizzen, horrified by the course of events, decided to escape the war and save his family by adopting a false Jewish identity and moving to England. Thus the Skizzens became the Fixels and Nita changed her name to Miriam.

Nita/Miriam is a typical, if not perfect, nostalgic. She suffers immensely because of the departure from her home country and the change of her name, identity and religion. Deprived of her old self, Nita/Miriam feels like an uprooted tree—weak and abandoned. In the United States, where she moved with the children after the war, she becomes even less able to restore her old self. For her, it is very closely linked to the place of her origin—Austria in general and the town of Graz in particular. According to Boym, nostalgia is less the longing for a place than for a specific time in the past (xv). In Miriam's case, these two notions can hardly be separated: for her, time and space merge into a single whole that is irreversibly lost under the pressure of history. Miriam's nostalgia is rooted in her recollection as a specific zone of memory. According to Assmann,

> The power of recollection works on existing material with a great degree of latitude . . . . Recollection does not heal the wounds, but softens them. This formative power is, of course, accompanied by the danger that it will take on a life of its own . . . . At its center, recollection harbors pain and irredeemable guilt. It is from this hidden source that specters of the past emerge at their own bidding, which cannot be controlled by rational consciousness. (83–84)

In London, as the nightmare of the war continues, she tells her children idyllic stories about the quiet village, cozy cottages and simple life of honest people, and her narratives are so emotional that they fill with colors, shapes and sounds:

> She painted cockcrow and sunset on a postcard and mailed it to their imagination. She made them hear fresh milk spilling in the pail. Woodpiles grew orderly and large while they listened. Flowers crowded the mountain trails and deer posed in glades cut by streams whose serene demeanor was periodically shattered by leaps of trout that only lacked for lemon. (Gass 33–34)

The logic of intimate recollection excludes critical evaluation of the past, which makes it psychologically very convenient for a displaced person. For Miriam it not only softens the wounds of misplacement, but also offers consolation as it allows for unrestricted subjectivity. Miriam's method of recollection rejects the principle of recording with subsequent preserving and retrieving. Instead, it generates emotions that become a founding principle of her permanently nostalgic state of mind. The reader is offered the polished and manicured image of *felix Austria* that has more to do with the imagination than with any recognizable historical past. Simple and idyllic life in Graz becomes even more idealized over time and the fact that Miriam never revisits her home country helps her maintain the image of romantic past remote from the reality of her present life. To a certain extent, it is even a second-degree "memory of past memories." For Skizzen's mother, nostalgia is expressed both in temporal and geographic terms: she misses her lost imagined Austria and the golden age when her life was simple, predictable and full of everyday joy. Miriam expresses her feelings about the old home country in a down-to-earth, if not outright primitive, way: "All Austrians dressed warmly, loved music, and, though they may have thought poorly of others, thought well of God. Now that the empire was gone, they lived happily by themselves and on their own. They toiled without complaining, but they also knew how to eat, drink and have fun. They prided themselves on being overweight" (Gass 10). Thus, the Austria of the past is imprinted on her memory and functions as an emotional, psychological and social frame for any new experience that anyway will not fit. No matter how hard anyone may try to help her take new roots, America will always remain "this country" as opposed to "back at home" where people, the scenery and even food were not only better, but more natural and healthier. Natural, healthy, safe, green and happy are the adjectives Miriam usually uses whenever she speaks with a painful sense of loss about her Austrian youth and adolescence.

Her existence is literally "canned" in the Austrian past. The American "segment" of her life has been much longer and less troubled, but still nostalgia does not allow her to develop emotionally and psychologically in her new environment and even though with the time she gets used to her whereabouts in the States, she always feels an alien there. What Miriam misses most from her Austrian past is not a specific place or period of time. She simply longs for the "slower rhythms of the past, for continuity, social cohesion and tradition" (Boym 16), something her life in the States cannot provide her.

The simplicity of Miriam's way of remembering her past is in fact quite misleading. If we refer to Assmann's classification of memory, Miriam's by definition is an inhabited memory, as it is connected with a specific carrier (an individual) who "proceeds selectively by remembering and forgetting" and "provides values that can support identity and norms" (Assmann 123). Inhabited memory can be otherwise called functional and as such is highly selective, giving presence only to a segment of memory's contents, and setting a boundary between "chosen, interpreted, and appropriated elements—that is, those that are attached to the configuration of the story" and "the amorphous mass of unattached elements" (Assmann 125). However, nostalgia does not allow Miriam to build a bridge between the past, present and future (and according to Assmann's classification this is one of the key characteristics of inhabited memory), as it uses the past to block the perception of both the present and future. Miriam's attitude toward her past is a good illustration that "nostalgia is not always about the past; it can be retrospective but also prospective. Fantasies of the past determined by needs of the present have a direct impact on realities of the future" (Boym xvi). On the other hand, Miriam's nostalgia "freezes" the past and does not allow for its productive re-thinking and re-evaluation.

Just as in *Double Vision*, language functions as an important memory stabilizer in *Middle C*—Miriam uses many German words when she speaks about life in the old country (names of dishes, clothes, words describing everyday routines). The German words always emerge when she praises life in Austria. In fact, she never manages to learn English well, and perhaps willingly speaks it with a heavy accent and numerous mistakes. As Assmann notes, individual memories are not only stabilized but also socialized by language (239). Abish's use of German words to describe the everyday realities of Viennese life adds a sentimental tinge to his memories and translates his experience into the reader's cultural and social language. Apparently, Miriam's disparate German words perform a similar function, although a strong nostalgic orientation captures and locks her past in its own separate world and does not allow the linguistic signs to help the reader share her experience and partake in her emotions.

One might argue that Abish and Gass created two different models of thinking about lost home that bring memory into play as a key principle of reading the past. While Abish brings together his impressions of a recent visit to Vienna as a renowned American writer in the late 1980s and fragments of memories of his early childhood in the city before the *Anschluss*, Gass creates in his work of fiction a typical idealized image of the Austrian province that Nita/Miriam Skizzen cherishes and takes with her to the United States. The double perspective in Abish's warm and slightly sentimental memoir is full of observations and critical speculations about the late twentieth-century Vienna, its residents, and their attitude to the past. In this portrait of the old and new Vienna, artistic urbanism entwines with personal memoirs linked to the place. A child's perspective imposed on the vision of a mature adult writer creates an atmospheric urban image marked with amazement, disappointment and expectations. Abish's "double vision" of Vienna, a palimpsest of memories and current impressions, shows how echoes of the past may affect and challenge the contemporary perspective, but at the same time does not allow the past to dominate the present.

For the character of Gass's novel, the town of Graz as her small *Heimat* is the emotional center of her American life and precludes the acceptance of reality. The simple and idyllic life in Austria becomes even more idealized over time and the fact that Miriam never revisits her home country helps her maintain the image of a detached, sentimentalized past that American life makes more and more unrealistic. The feeling of nostalgia for the charming world of peace and clear values of the former Austrian home is integrated into the American identity-making of the character and makes Miriam feel an eternal alien.

The semi-fictional (twice-seen) Austria of Walter Abish and the fictional (twice-removed) Austria of William H. Gass are both unreal countries, though unreal in two different ways. In Abish's *Double Vision*, the memory of Vienna is not merely functional—it is live, critical, and somehow capable of integration with the present. It is quite open and does not block a different reading of the city as a place that remembers. On the contrary, for the protagonist of Gass's *Middle C*, the memory of adolescence and youth in Graz is dominated by nostalgia that, in her case, functions, to summon Boym's categories one last time, less as a creative emotion and more as a social disease that blocks the present and future and precludes any critical thinking about past experiences.

WORKS CITED

Abish, Walter. *Double Vision.* New York: Alfred A. Knopf, 2004.

Assmann, Aleida. *Cultural Memory and Western Civilization. Functions, Media, Archives*. New York: Cambridge UP, 2011.

Benjamin, Walter. *The Work of Art in the Age of Its Technological Reproductivity, and Other Writings on Media.* Eds. Michael W. Jennings, Brigid Doherty and Thomas Y. Levin. Cambridge: Harvard UP, 2008.

Boym, Svetlana. *The Future of Nostalgia.* New York: Basic Books, 2001.

Gass, William H. *Middle C.* New York: Alfred A. Knopf, 2013.

CONTRIBUTORS

Marty Gecek is the chair of the Salzburg Seminar American Studies Association and director of American Studies symposia at Salzburg Global Seminar. With the help and advice of her Advisory Board, she chooses the annual program theme, which addresses some aspect of the study of America, including the areas of literature, foreign policy, history, cultural studies and popular culture. She invites appropriate faculty members, disseminates program materials to contacts around the world, and is responsible for the selection of attendees. The Association is self-supporting and she helps to raise funding for scholarships. Ms. Gecek joined the Salzburg Global Seminar in 1966, and has held a number of positions at the institution, including office manager, associate director for administration and personnel, and associate director of the American Studies Center. She holds a B.A. in sociology from Hollins University, Virginia.

Walter Grünzweig, a native of Graz, Austria, is professor of American literature and culture at TU Dortmund University. He specializes on nineteenth-century American literary and culture, transatlantic relations and international education. He has been working on and with Carl Djerassi since the second half of the 1990s.

Jeanne C. Holland received her Ph.D. in American Studies from the University of Hawai'i, Manoa. Her dissertation focused on why Freud was well received by the New England intellectual community at the beginning of the twentieth century. Professor Holland was a Fulbright Professor at the University of Jyväskylä, Finland and the University of Salzburg, Austria. She was a full professor, Dean and Provost at Finlandia University, Michigan, and Dean of the College of International Studies, Hawai'i Pacific University, Honolulu. Her research interests are intellectual history, gender studies, and American government. Retired from full-time academic work, she is currently a Senior Teaching Fellow at the University of Nevada, Las Vegas.

Dean J. Kotlowski is professor of history at Salisbury University, Maryland, USA. He received his B.A. from Canisius College and his M.A. and Ph.D. from Indiana University Bloomington. He is the author of *Nixon's Civil*

Rights: Politics, Principle, and Policy (Harvard University Press, 2001) and *Paul V. McNutt and the Age of FDR* (Indiana University Press, 2015) and the editor of *The European Union: From Jean Monnet to the Euro* (Ohio University Press, 2000). He has published over thirty articles and book chapters in the United States, United Kingdom, Australia, Austria, Germany, Denmark, Finland, and Russia. He has been a Fulbright scholar in the Philippines (2008) and Austria (2016), and a visiting fellow at the Humanities Research Centre, Australian National University.

Marta Koval is a Professor of American Literature at the Institute of English and American Studies, University of Gdansk, Poland. She teaches courses on contemporary American fiction and culture. Her academic interests include postwar American fiction, fictional representation of memory and nostalgia, and transformations of the historical novel in the late twentieth to early twenty-first century. She is the author of many essays on post WWII American fiction. She has published two books - *Play in the Novel, Playing the Novel: On John Barth's Fiction* (2000) and *"We Search the Past ... for Our Own Lost Selves." Representations of Historical Experience in Recent American Fiction* (2013). She visited Michigan State University as a Senior Fulbright scholar in 2004-2005.

Yuval Lubin is a Master's student in the Department of English at the Hebrew University of Jerusalem concentrating on modernist literature. His interests include the role of comedy in modernist literature, the employment of carnival as a method of evaluation and critical comparison of film adaptations of literature to the source material. His research examines the representation of epistemological failure through comedy in *Moby Dick* and *The Third Policeman.* He is a graduate of the English department from the Hebrew University of Jerusalem with a minor in comparative literature. He has won the Teitelbaum Award for Excellence in the Novel and was a beneficiary of the German Learning Scholarship of the Europe Forum at Hebrew University.

Dante Mazzari is a Master's candidate at Georgetown University's School of Foreign Service, focusing on transatlantic economic and security issues. Prior to coming to Georgetown, he worked at the Organization for Security and Cooperation in Europe in Vienna and INTERPOL's general secretariat in Lyon, France. He has also done work for the German Marshall Fund of the

United State and the World Bank, both in Washington, DC. He is a native of Portsmouth, NH and holds a degree in international relations from the University of Edinburgh.

Joshua Parker is an assistant professor of American studies at the University of Salzburg, with research interests in place and space in American literature, transatlantic relations and narrative theory. His books include *Metamorphosis and Place* (2009), *Austria and America: Cross-Cultural Encounters 1865-1933* (2014), and *Tales of Berlin in American Literature up to the 21st Century* (2016).

Ralph J. Poole is professor of American studies at the University of Salzburg. His publications include a study on the Avant-Garde tradition in American theatre, a book on satirical and autoethnographical "cannibal" texts, and most recently a collection of essays on "dangerous masculinities." He currently conducts a project funded by the Austrian Science Fund on "Gender and Comedy in the Age of the American Revolution." His research interests include American literature, drama, gender/queer/masculinity studies, popular culture, and transatlantic negotiations.

Anne-Marie Scholz holds a teaching affiliation with the University of Bremen, Germany as a "Privatdozentin." Most recently, she was Adjunct Professor of North American Studies at the University of Konstanz. She has also taught at the Universities of Bonn, Hamburg, Tübingen and the University of California, Irvine. Her work has focused upon the transnational reception of American popular culture in Europe (and vice versa) as well as upon new theoretical and methodological approaches to film adaptation study. She is the author of *An Orgy of Propriety: Jane Austen and the Emergence and Legacy of the Female Author in America, 1826-1926* (Trier, 1999), and *From Fidelity to History: Film Adaptations as Cultural Events in the Twentieth Century* (Berghahn, 2013), as well as of numerous articles exploring the interdisciplinary relationship between film, literature and history. This is her third study of *The Third Man*.

Jonathan Singerton is currently completing a Ph.D. entitled "Empires on the Edge—The Habsburg Monarchy and the American Revolution, 1763-1789" at the University of Edinburgh under the primary supervision of Professor Francis D. Cogliano. He is also concurrently an Ernst Mach Fellow at the Institut für Neuzeit- und Zeitgeschichtsforschung at the Österreichische Akademie der Wissenschaften in Vienna under the supervision of Dr. William D. Godsey and was previously a short-term fellow at the International Center for Jefferson Studies. These alongside the generous funding from the Dietrich W. Botstiber Foundation has allowed him to conduct archival research on both sides of the Atlantic necessary for his study into the eighteenth-century connections between the Habsburg Monarchy and the emerging United States of America.

Bernhard Wenzl studied North-American literature at the University of Vienna and Université de Bourgogne in Dijon, France. He completed his M.A. studies with a thesis about the frontier myth in Willa Cather's pioneer novels and has been pursuing a Ph.D. project about memory in Ivan Doig's fiction. In 2008 he participated in an extensive study trip to the Canadian West, visiting universities in Manitoba, Alberta and British Columbia. His research focus is on American and Canadian fiction of the twentieth century. He has published papers and given presentations on John Dos Passos, Sinclair Lewis, John Marlyn, and Sinclair Ross. Currently he works as web editor at the Institute of Science and Technology Austria.